ONE EGG IS A FORTUNE

memories and recipes to share

COMPILED BY

Pnina Jacobson & Judy Kempler

DEDICATION

This book is lovingly dedicated to our families
~ Ivor, Sam, Danielle and Laura ~
~ John, Steven, Jacqui and Lise ~

our mothers Rhona and Evi (forever patient!)
and to the memory of our cherished fathers,
Sam and Felix, and grandparents.

CONTENTS

SOMETHING TO START 13

SOMETHING SAVOURY 75

SOMETHING SUBSTANTIAL 151

SOMETHING SWEET 217

BEGINNINGS

Sacramento
MARLENA SPIELER

San Raphael
MIRI EISEN

San Francisco
DENNIS ROSS

Los Angeles
RABBI SHMULEY BOTEACH

Morton Grove, Illinois
MARLEE MATLIN

Lexington
ETHAN ZOHN

Philadelphia
MARC SALEM

UNITED STATES OF AMERICA

Toronto
BARBARA KIRSHENBLATT-GIMBLETT
RACHAEL KOHN

Connecticut
RUTH HENDEL

New York
NESHAMA CARLEBACH
PHYLLIS CHESLER
ALAN DERSHOWITZ
TOVAH FELDSHUH
HERSCHAL HERSCHER
ART SPIEGELMAN
MICHAEL STEINHARDT

Antwerp
ISI LEIBLER

Wuppertal
GEORGE DREYFUS

Leeds
PROFESSOR ALAN CROWN

Leicester
ALAN GOLD

UNITED
KINGDOM

Cardiff
LORD JANNER

BELGIUM

GERM
A

SWITZERLAND

Bournemouth
MAX MARKSON

London
MARTIN INDYK
NAOMI LEIBLER

Zurich
MADELINE KUNIN

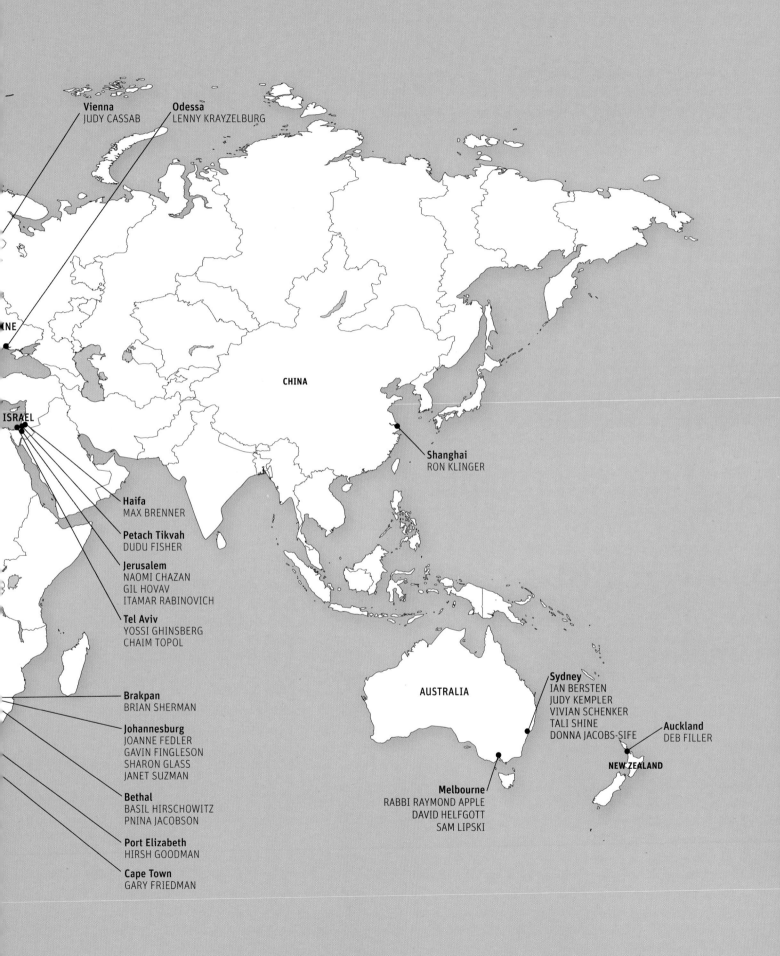

Vienna
JUDY CASSAB

Odessa
LENNY KRAYZELBURG

NE

ISRAEL

Haifa
MAX BRENNER

Petach Tikvah
DUDU FISHER

Jerusalem
NAOMI CHAZAN
GIL HOVAV
ITAMAR RABINOVICH

Tel Aviv
YOSSI GHINSBERG
CHAIM TOPOL

Brakpan
BRIAN SHERMAN

Johannesburg
JOANNE FEDLER
GAVIN FINGLESON
SHARON GLASS
JANET SUZMAN

Bethal
BASIL HIRSCHOWITZ
PNINA JACOBSON

Port Elizabeth
HIRSH GOODMAN

Cape Town
GARY FRIEDMAN

CHINA

Shanghai
RON KLINGER

AUSTRALIA

Sydney
IAN BERSTEN
JUDY KEMPLER
VIVIAN SCHENKER
TALI SHINE
DONNA JACOBS-SIFE

Auckland
DEB FILLER

NEW ZEALAND

Melbourne
RABBI RAYMOND APPLE
DAVID HELFGOTT
SAM LIPSKI

INTRODUCTION
Judy Kempler

'My earliest food memories stem from my grandparents' pantry, which was lined with jars of unusual homemade treats: rock-hard ginger biscuits, cumquat jam made of fruits harvested from the neighbour's trees and hand-picked and dried Blue Mountains mushrooms. My father came from a very large, close-knit family; his parents were migrants from Vienna and they always had a story to tell about life in their home country. As my brother, cousins and I grew older we became part of the stories – the gathering of wild berries and mushrooms that was part of my grandparents' youth ...We were taught to pick only one sort of mushroom, to ensure that no poisonous ones were brought home. It was dense yellow with a sticky, shiny brown skin, found under the fallen needles of pine trees. The stems had to be cut with a sharp knife so they would grow again. I can still hear the triumphant screeches that accompanied a mushroom discovery! I have continued to share these types of experiences with my own family.'

One Egg Is A Fortune is more than a recipe collection; it is a book full of heart, an anthology of cultural vignettes with food as the central motif, showing that food is a great equaliser.

Jewish people have a great love of storytelling. Memories of joyous times are just as important to record and pass on as are tales of suffering. Food has always been central to Jewish life; it holds both biblical and historical significance and often reflects our heritage. Through circumstances often not of our choosing, Jews have been wanderers, forced to move from place to place. With migration, we adopted the food of our new homes, fusing it with traditional Jewish cuisine.

Fifty well-known Jewish figures from around the world have contributed recipes and anecdotes to *One Egg Is A Fortune*, showcasing the diversity of contemporary Jewish life. And while each person tells a unique story, their anecdotes reveal that the enjoyment of food is the common thread that binds us together. The title of our book was inspired by one of these beautiful stories.

The genesis of this book began many years ago. Pnina and I met when our children were young. Standing at the bus stop seeing our kids off to school, we would often talk about doing something worthwhile for the community and yet still be stay-at-home mothers, caring for our families. As we got talking, we realised that we shared an interest in food and a curiosity about the way our childhood memories influenced the recipes we created as adults. It seemed a good idea to combine our love of cooking and storytelling in a book. At this time, I was a carer for my late mother-in-law Viola, and I realised that so much more was needed to care for our ageing community. We decided then that part of the proceeds from our book would support Jewish aged care.

In order to create something a little unusual yet valuable, Pnina and I sought contributions worldwide. We contacted so many people, at all hours of the day and night, and sometimes it took six months or more to get an acceptance, a maybe, or even a rejection. The challenges of everyday life, together with learning how to publish a book, forged a lifelong friendship. The assembly of *One Egg Is A Fortune* represents a journey of over ten years and sincere thanks go to the contributors, who gave so generously of their time.

As cooking and food appreciation have become popular pastimes, there are now more cookbooks than ever. However, this collection is different and very special. Besides being a cookbook, *One Egg Is A Fortune* is a snapshot and a social record of Jewish communities all over the world. The stories are heartfelt and heart-warming, and the recipes are delicious. We hope you will enjoy them – and pass them on to future generations.

Fifty well-known Jewish figures from around the world have contributed recipes and anecdotes to 'One Egg Is A Fortune', showcasing the diversity of contemporary Jewish life. And while each person tells a unique story, their anecdotes reveal that the enjoyment of food is the common thread that binds us together. The title of our book was inspired by one of these beautiful stories.

It may be hard to imagine a time when our parents and friends grow old; many of us will find we are called on to assist in their care. In purchasing this book, you are helping to raise extra and much-needed funds to ensure the aged in our community get the best from life.

One Egg Is A Fortune is available from www.oneeggisafortune.com or selected booksellers and outlets.

ACKNOWLEDGMENTS

We gratefully acknowledge that this book has only been made possible through the generosity of our contributors and their staff and families – thank you.

Special mention must go to our husbands who have been delighted that our many hours together have avoided huge credit card debts!

Special mention to our children, our honest food critics and guinea pigs. This book would not have eventuated without our resident IT specialist, Steven.

Special mention to our mums who are forever patient and encouraged us to finally finish. Yes, you can now tell everyone what your daughter has been doing with her time!

To Alan Gold, an incredibly enthusiastic and supportive mentor and friend, who not only believed in us, but in the value of our book. Pure Gold!

To Helen Smith, for your continuous kindness and assistance.

To all our family and friends, too numerous to mention by name, who at different stages have helped create our book and wondered for so long what we were doing: our sincerest thanks. Many generously shared their favourite recipes (included in the Extra Recipes sections) and for this we are very grateful.

~

We were privileged to work with dedicated and caring professionals:

Craig Cranko, our highly talented photographer, exuded serenity, kindness and warmth – all of which is reflected in his work. Craig is a freelance commercial photographer who specialises in food, product, portrait and other photography.

Michele Cranston, our gorgeous food stylist with the most beautiful smile and patience, prepared and presented our recipes with simplicity and flair, always using the freshest produce available. Her wealth of experience in cooking, catering, writing and creating has made her one of the world's best-selling cookbook authors.

Melanie Feddersen, our exceptionally patient and enthusiastic book designer – despite our unforseen hurdles, her gentle manner, guidance and professionalism saw us through. Melanie's talent and her creativity shines through our beautiful book.

Nadine Davidoff, our efficient editor, ever-attentive to detail, enriched our manuscript and had an immediate understanding of our needs. Nadine Davidoff is a freelance book editor and consultant.

Jirsch Sutherland IP, for their legal assistance.

Something to Start

- Pickled Herring & Tomato Bruschetta
- Vegetable Terrine 'Encased' in Spinach
- Deb's Challah
- Romanian Eggplant Salad with Figs & Antipasto
- Kichel
- Fresh Blood-Orange Marmalade
- Pear & Ginger Jam
- Dora's Leek, Barley & Split Pea Soup
- Passover Bagels
- Fresh Tomato Soup
- Kapusniak
- Carrot Tzimmes Soufflé
- Fish Quenelles with Two Sauces
- Asparagus Teriyaki
- Chicken & Corn Soup
- Brie En Cocotte
- Lentil Soup with Garlic & Cumin
- Chicken Consommé with Pesto Chicken Dumplings
- French Onion Soup
- Gazpacho
- Papas Rellenas (Stuffed Potatoes)
- Potato Curry Puffs
- Rice Paper Spring Rolls
- Spinach Soup
- Watermelon & Feta Bites

GEORGE DREYFUS

George Dreyfus AM is a
composer and conductor
of classical and
contemporary music.

He was born in 1928 in Wuppertal, Germany, and grew
up in a home surrounded by culture with his parents
Alfred and Hilde, and his brother Richard. Due to
unsettling times, the family moved to Berlin in 1935
where George started to learn the piano. In 1939,
they escaped to Australia and for a while George and
his brother lived in the Melbourne children's home
Larino until the family moved into a unit in St Kilda.

Piano lessons, singing in the synagogue choir,
conducting the school choir at Melbourne High, making
a gramophone record, and giving talks on Richard
Strauss were just some of George's extracurricular
interests when growing up. His music career began as
a bassoonist with TC Williamson's Theatres in 1948,
followed by the Melbourne Symphony Orchestra from
1953–54 and 1958–64. He began composing full-time
in 1965 and became the 'Mr New Music' of Melbourne.
He has formed contemporary music performing
groups and been awarded travel grants, fellowships,
residencies and commissions.

George is the recipient of many prizes, including
the 1967 ANU Creative Arts Fellowship and the 1974
Best Performance for an Australian Instrumental award
for the bestselling theme single *Rush*. In 1992 George
was awarded the Member of the Order of Australia for
his services to music, and in 2002 the Bundesverdienst
Kreuz from the Federal German Republic.

Living in Melbourne, Australia, with his family,
George continues to compose, conduct and
perform today.

Arm Yourself with Noseplugs!

Before I begin, I need to make one thing clear: I can't cook. It's not that I have no talent with food, it's not that I have no love for the softly simmering saucepan, the aroma of burnt toast or the delectable delights of the delicatessen at Camberwell market. I just can't be bothered.

I remember with great affection when my son Jonathan and I decided to heat up a croissant under the griller. Ten minutes later when the smoke detector went off we rushed into the kitchen, pulled out the griller tray to find flames reaching the ceiling. Needless to say, once we'd doused the blaze, there wasn't much left of the croissant.

I have a predilection for smelly fish. Let me tell you about the time when Jonathan walked into the house, took one deep breath and walked out again; I had decided to make *eingelegte heringe,* pickled herrings. Several cans of Fragrance of Nature later, he agreed to come back in again. Now I only make *eingelegte heringe* when he is away at *Netzer* youth camp.

I do have good cooking ventures such as spaghetti bolognaise; my fish and chips are top of the range; and no one has been able to cap my soft serves. I only require one ingredient: my wallet.

Recipe: *Eingelegte Heringe*

Drive to Camberwell market, extract salted herring direct from barrel at delicatessen, take home, clean and soak overnight, *einlegen* (immerse) in vinegar, onion rings, peppercorns, bay-leaves; it's not exactly what you'd call cooking. Leave for two or three days and then: enjoy!

George's warning: Do not attempt this operation unless armed with earthenware pot *zum einlegen*.

Jonathan's warning: Do not attempt this operation unless armed with noseplugs and a large can of Fragrance of Nature.

Pickled Herring & Tomato Bruschetta

A composition from the market

pickled herring
tomato topping
1 loaf Italian bread, such as ciabatta
1 large clove garlic, peeled
olive oil, to drizzle

PICKLED HERRING
250g premium matjes herring fillets
2 medium white onions, sliced
1¼ cups white sugar
2 cups white vinegar

½ teaspoon freshly ground black pepper
3 bay leaves
20 black peppercorns

TOMATO TOPPING
2 cloves garlic, finely chopped
2 large tomatoes, seeded and diced
1 tablespoon olive oil
2 tablespoons vinegar, white or balsamic
salt and freshly ground black pepper
sprigs of flat-leaf parsley

Make herring: Rinse and dry herring fillets. Cut each fillet into 5 even-sized pieces. In a glass jar or container, layer herring pieces and sliced onions. Combine remaining ingredients and pour over herring and onions. Seal and place into refrigerator for two days.

Make toppings: Mix the garlic, tomato, olive oil and vinegar together in a bowl and set aside. Adjust seasoning with salt and black pepper. Cut pickled herrings and onions into tiny pieces (same size as the diced tomatoes).

Make bruschetta: Preheat oven to 200°C. Cut bread into diagonal 1cm slices and place on a baking tray. Bake for a few minutes until lightly golden. Rub top side of each slice with garlic clove and lightly drizzle with olive oil.

Place the prepared bread slices on a serving platter. Spoon tomato mixture over half the bread and herring mixture on the other half. Place a sprig of parsley on top.

Note: Bruschetta are at their best when made at the last moment to keep the bread from drying out or the toppings from making the bread soggy.

(SERVES 6–8)

TOVAH FELDSHUH

Tovah Feldshuh is an acclaimed actor and cabaret performer and has appeared in Broadway productions, on television and in movies.

Tovah was born in 1952 in New York to immigrant parents from Minsk, Russia. Under the name of Terri Fairchild, and with her signature flaming red hair, she began her career as a rock singer. Tovah is a graduate of Sarah Lawrence College and has taught acting at Yale, Cornell and New York universities.

For her work on the New York stage in *Yentl, Sarava, Lend Me a Tenor* and *Golda's Balcony,* Tovah has earned four Tony nominations for Best Actress and won four Drama Desk awards (including one for *Golda's Balcony*), four Outer Critics Circle awards, and the Obie. *Golda's Balcony,* the one-woman show about Golda Meir, is the longest-running one-woman show in Broadway history. Tovah also won the 2003 Lucille Lortel Award for Best Actress for *Golda's Balcony.* In 2005, Tovah received an EPIC Award, dedicated to advancing women's leadership, from the White House Project for this play.

Tovah is a supporter of Seeds of Peace, a non-profit, non-political organisation that helps teenagers from regions of conflict. She is the recipient of the Eleanor Roosevelt Humanities Award and the Israel Peace Medal.

Tovah lives in New York with her husband Andrew. They have two children, Garson Brandon and Amanda Claire.

Jewish Penicillin

We had a kosher-style wedding at the Plaza Hotel when Andrew and I were married. The Plaza catering staff erroneously delivered a huge vat of shrimp to our *hors d'oeuvres* hour. The guests were scandalised for about two seconds before descending on that shrimp like a pack of wolves. It was all gone within two shakes of a lamb's tail! We were not in the room when the shrimp arrived, but I must say that it was heartily enjoyed by all! Thankfully, there were no pig's trotters on the main course and everything else went smoothly. Incidentally, we were not charged for the shrimp.

The opening line from the show *Golda's Balcony* is, 'I know you think of me as Mama-le-Golda, who makes chicken soup for her soldiers...' Golda Meir, the prime minister of Israel from 1969–74, not only made chicken soup for her soldiers but she also baked very good *schnecken,* sweet spiral-shaped pastries. Her ministers would meet around her green formica kitchen table and discuss the affairs of state while Golda served this pastry with coffee as they tried to solve the crises of the nation.

We all know that chicken soup has long been known as the universal cure-all – the Jewish penicillin. After all, our moms and grandmas have been saying so forever. In almost every part of the world, a bowl of steaming hot chicken soup is an antidote for a sore finger, colds and flu, depression, bad report cards, upset stomachs, political turmoil, allergies, respiratory disorders, arthritis and scraped knees.

For me, the fat content in the soup is what makes it so healthy. Even after most of the fat has been skimmed off, the remnants still envelop the vocal chords. This wonderful non-acid coating stays on the back of your throat so that anything that is frayed or irritated is smoothed over and soothed. It's like putting your hand into warm paraffin. Chicken soup is a meal in itself and during the run of *Golda's Balcony* in New York, I had my mother's chicken soup every day. With over six hundred performances, that's a lot of chicken soup!

Vegetable Terrine 'Encased' in Spinach

'My mother was eating derma *at a wedding on the evening of 26 December. A few hours later, I was born at 2.00 am. She often credited the* derma *for the labour ... a riot!' — Tovah Feldshuh*

This European delicacy, known as derma *or* kishke, *was usually made from beef casings stuffed with a seasoned mixture of meat, flour, onions, vegetables and chicken fat, boiled and then roasted. Here is a contemporary vegetarian version which can be served cold or reheated, plain or with a lemon and dill mayonnaise.*

8–10 large fresh silverbeet/spinach leaves, washed and white stalks discarded

3 medium carrots, roughly chopped

300g kumara or orange sweet potato, roughly chopped

1 teaspoon olive oil

½ small white onion, roughly chopped

½ vegetable stock cube

salt and white pepper, to taste

3–4 tablespoons plain flour

3–4 large eggs

3 medium potatoes, peeled and roughly chopped

200g cauliflower, broken into tiny florets

200g celery (2½ stalks), stringed and sliced

1 tablespoon parsley

2 large zucchini, grated

Each layer of the terrine makes a quantity of approximately 1½ cups of blended vegetables. Preheat oven to 150°C. Line base and sides of a 25mm x 100mm x 70mm terrine/loaf tin with baking paper and spray with oil. Prepare a *bain marie,* a large baking dish half-filled with water, for terrine to sit in whilst baking.

Wilt silverbeet in boiling water and gently squeeze to remove excess liquid. Line base of terrine with the longest leaf, overhanging the edges so that it can be folded over top for sealing when filled. Repeat the process in the other direction until the entire terrine has been lined. Reserve three extra leaves for layering.

Layer 1: Boil carrots and kumara until soft. Drain. Heat oil in frying pan and sauté onions until translucent. Puree carrots, kumara, onions, stock cube and pepper and set aside. Stir through 1 tablespoon flour and 1 egg until smooth. Pour into terrine and spread evenly. Place a silverbeet leaf over and press down to make sure layer is level.

Layer 2: Boil potatoes until soft, drain, puree, season with salt and white pepper and set aside. Boil cauliflower until tender and drain. Stir through 1 tablespoon flour and 1 egg until smooth and gently mix through the cauliflower. Pour into terrine and spread evenly. Place a spinach leaf over and gently press down to make sure layer is level.

Layer 3: Boil celery, squeeze out water, season with salt and pepper, puree with parsley and set aside. Blanch the zucchini, squeeze out water and stir through celery. Stir through 1–2 tablespoons flour and 1–2 eggs, depending on how liquid the consistency is. Pour mixture into terrine and spread evenly. Place a spinach leaf over and gently press down. Fold overhanging spinach leaves over the terrine to seal. Place terrine in *bain marie* and bake for 1 hour. Allow to cool and refrigerate until ready to serve.

(SERVES 8–10 AS A STARTER OR 4–5 AS A MAIN)

DEB FILLER

Deb Filler is a world-famous actor, writer and comic.

Her critically acclaimed performances have included sold-out shows in New York, Berlin, London, Edinburgh, Montreal, Washington, Australia, and her homeland, New Zealand. In 2005 she was nominated for a Helen Hayes Award for Outstanding Actress for her solo piece, *Filler Up!*

Deb continues to work on creating new shows, and a book, *Filler Up! Food on a Schtick: Recipes and Stories from a South Pacific Jewish Family*. The slowly simmering book will be 'fillered up' with delicious recipes from her family and her travels throughout the world.

Currently based in Toronto, Canada, but still strongly connected to New Zealand and New York, Deb's family and their Holocaust experiences have inspired much of her work. Her characters, like many of us, are true survivors.

The Anti-Liver/Pro-Schnitzel Party

My sister and I were obliged to eat liver as kids because that's what a healthy family ate. And our mum did what a lot of people do: she cooked that offal 'til it could just about walk off the table on its own. I ask you, what's to like about eating pungent styrofoam? One thing was clear: I chose my path in life and I chose it early ... I was in the anti-liver/pro-schnitzel party.

One night Mum tried to get one over on us. She told us to relax, sit and watch TV in the lounge room while she prepared our favourite ... the precious schnitzel and potato salad. Oh yes, we *could* watch *The Jetsons!* She closed the door to the kitchen. I turned to my sister and said, 'Something's up!'

Eager for her favourite meal, my sister soon lost herself in the search for George Jetson's new space scooter while I remained stoically suspicious. Then the smell came wafting down our hallway and into the lounge – a dead giveaway. Overcooked *liver!* We were being suckered. Mother waltzed in with trays of schnitzel presented with a parsley curl and wedge of lemon. I knew this was a strategic moment. But what should we do? If we made a stand would we come out worse off than when we started? No kid won against their mother in 1965.

I turned to my sister and whispered, 'We've been duped!'

'Wahh? This! It's *liver schnitzel!*'

'NOOOO!'

It was definitely our biggest sister-bonding moment. And no matter how much lemon juice or tomato sauce we used, nothing would *ivah, ivah* disguise that taste or smell.

We turned off *The Jetsons* and listened. In the kitchen our mum was humming and our dad was complimenting her on her miraculous dinner. Slowly, carefully, we tiptoed out of the lounge, down the hallway, out the front door and into the front garden. We knew that if we were discovered, we'd have to eat liver for the rest of our lives.

Would she hear us? What could we do if she did? We stood side by side on the front lawn and on a count, with all our might, we grasped our liver schnitzels and flung them as hard as frisbees into the main road. They were chewed by the tyres of the oncoming traffic. Consumed at last!

I suspect that to this day, my sister and I are the only people in Mt Roskill to ever hear the sound of liver schnitzel flapping under the chassis of a Triumph Herald.

'We're finished Mum!'

'Girls, your plates, they're clean! You liked it?'

'No. It wasn't your normal schnitzel. So please don't *ivah* make it again.'

And, bless her, to this day she never has.

Deb's Challah
My grandmother's recipe — a show-stopper!

1 cup sugar

2¾ cups warm water

1 envelope dried yeast (2 teaspoons)

4 tablespoons light vegetable oil

4 teaspoons salt

2 free-range eggs, lightly beaten

7–8 cups flour

1 egg yolk beaten with 1 teaspoon water
 (egg wash)

poppy/sesame seeds

Rinse a large mixing bowl with hot water. Using this warm bowl, dissolve 1 teaspoon of sugar in the warm water. Sprinkle the yeast on top and leave to stand for 10 minutes. Stir to dissolve. Add oil, remaining sugar, salt and eggs and beat well. Add three cups of flour at a time until all flour is mixed. Dough should be sticky.

Cover dough and let rest for 10 minutes. Turn out onto a floured board and knead for 10 minutes, adding flour as needed.

Clean and lightly oil mixing bowl. Place dough back into bowl, cover with a damp cloth and leave in a warm place for about 2 hours, until doubled in bulk. Punch down and allow dough – covered, in a warm place for 45 minutes – to rise again. Punch down again. At this stage dough can be divided to make two medium-sized loaves or one large loaf.

Divide dough into three equal parts and roll into tubular shapes by hand. Braid the three pieces together ensuring that the ends are secured and tucked under. Place on a lightly greased baking sheet. Cover with a damp cloth and let rise in a warm place until doubled, about 45 minutes. Preheat oven to 200°C.

Brush loaf with egg wash and sprinkle with poppy seeds. Bake for about 30 minutes, until deep golden brown.

Notes: To freeze dough, cover securely with plastic wrap. To prepare dough ahead of baking, place dough in a well-oiled bowl, cover with wax paper and a damp cloth and refrigerate for up to 5 days, ensuring the cloth stays damp. When ready to use, frozen or refrigerated, allow to come to room temperature and double in size again. Proceed with the recipe.

(MAKES 2 BRAIDED BREAD LOAVES)

Mama would carefully choose the eggplants, selecting the soft ones rather than the perky shimmering ones.

From the mountains to the sea, Israel is a land of milk and honey...

YOSSI GHINSBERG

Yossi Ghinsberg is an author and motivational speaker. He was born in 1959 in Israel.

Like many Israelis, Yossi went backpacking after his military service, deciding to travel to South America. *Jungle*, an account of his harrowing adventures and survival, was published in 1986 and translated into eight languages. Yossi studied philosophy and business at Tel Aviv University with further studies in Kabbalah (Jewish mysticism) and other religious and philosophical teachings.

Yossi returned to the Amazon in 1992 to initiate The Chalalan Project to teach the indigenous people how to simultaneously conserve the environment and sustain themselves. This has won him international acclaim. In 1995 he was appointed vice-president of the Center for Investigation and Treatment of Addiction (CITA), established for the treatment of opiate addiction. At the peak of the intifada (Israeli–Palestinian conflict) in 2001, Yossi was invited to organise a reconciliation festival in Israel. Despite the escalation of violence in the region, the festival was a huge success, attracting Jewish and Muslim spiritual leaders.

Yossi's book, *The Laws of the Jungle: Jaguars Don't Need Self Help Books*, is an inspirational book of reflection upon the natural world.

He lives in the hinterlands of Byron Bay, Australia, Israel and the UK. He is married to Belinda and they have four children, Mia, Cayam, Nissim and Shalem.

The Alchemist in the Kitchen

My father had old-fashioned values and did not approve of my mother going out to work. So she stayed at home amongst the pots and pans in the kitchen, the never-ending household maintenance, and her long clacking knitting needles.

Mama was born in Kelerash, a small town on the border of Bulgaria and Romania, the youngest of four daughters. Her name was Stela. Her older sisters, Jentila, Rara and Berta, were born to a different mother. When their mother passed away, my grandpa married her cousin from Bulgaria to take care of the girls; that cousin was my grandma.

In 1951, my parents migrated to Israel from Romania. They felt very fortunate for they had survived the war and were now living amongst Jews in a democracy. A year later my brother Moshe was born in a village in the Upper Galilee. These were new experiences and my mother was nothing but grateful. My father, however, found this new life very difficult, often complaining, sometimes regretting their migration and suggesting that we should move to Canada where life would be easier. But Mama, a true Zionist, refused to even hear of it; she loved Israel. These early days of the emerging state, also known as the *Tzena*, were years of economic hardship and shortages where people lived on food rations. Moshe was lucky if he tasted milk and eggs once a week.

But in a short time, the arid deserts flowered into orchards and fields yielding an abundance of biblical proportions. Israel indeed became the land of milk and honey, just as the spies had reported back to Moses in Sinai.

Despite the hardships, my mother missed the *Tzena* days; she said it was the most beautiful time of her life. She recalled people gathering on street corners and dancing the *hora*. When she craved something extra special to eat, she would cut a fresh hot chilli pepper into thin rings, cover it with a thick layer of soybean oil, sprinkle it with coarse salt and into this dip freshly cut wholemeal bread, relishing it with joy. When I miss my mother, I make myself this simple dish – nothing tastes better.

Mama had other such idiosyncrasies. She was a master pickler. Nothing would be safe from her jars; she would even pickle watermelon skin! She was passionate about Bulgarian cheese, which is similar to feta, keeping it in brine to maintain its moisture. In our house everything was eaten with the cheese – melons and grapes, eggplant dishes, salads, and the famous Romanian polenta staple *memelige*. Mama would even throw cheese crumbs into her cup of tea! The aroma of her baking *buikitikos*, little Bulgarian pastries with melted kashkaval cheese ...

clockwise from top left: Yossi's mother Stela; brother Moshe, Yossi and Stela; Yossi's parents; Stela with her older sisters.

Mama would even throw cheese crumbs into her cup of tea! The aroma of her baking buikitikos, little Bulgarian pastries with melted kashkaval cheese ... just the thought of them brings back memories. What wouldn't I give to taste her treats once again!

just the thought of them brings back memories. What wouldn't I give to taste her treats once again!

Yet of all dishes, there was one we ate daily and sometimes even twice a day – eggplant salad Romanian-style. This was the signature dish of the house and a meal wasn't a meal without it. Mama would carefully choose the eggplants, selecting the soft ones rather than the perky shimmering ones. My job was to pierce the eggplants with a fork to prevent them from exploding when we cooked them. Mama would place two eggplants on top of each gas burner and turn them from side to side, bottom and top until their skin burnt and their body collapsed oozing their oily juices. The flames gave them their distinct smell and taste. The eggplants would then be washed under cold water, meticulously peeled to separate the burnt skin from the opaque yellowish-brown flesh. The vegetable was placed in a colander to rest, cool and drain off the bitterness. After being placed in a blender on the slowest speed, Mama would gradually add the oil and salt, nothing else. The transformation was miraculous. The dark yellowish bulk of eggplant flesh would turn white and bright, perfectly smooth and appetising to look at. To serve, she would place a large scoop of eggplant salad in the middle of a plate and garnish it with finely chopped onions that were as perfect as tiny diamonds. She decorated the edge of the plate with alternating wedges of tomatoes and black olives. A generous slice of Bulgarian cheese was placed right in the middle and finally a bold sprinkle of oil to finish the dish – perfection! Mama was a true alchemist! Both my sister-in-law and I have tried our best to reproduce this same taste, but we can't. There's magic to it and it's not in the ingredients or the method but in the hand.

Sadly, my mama has Alzheimer's disease and lives in a home. Although she doesn't recognise me, she smiles when I ask if she has prepared my favourite eggplant salad. Amongst the other patients is an old Yemenite lady, and I have come to know her son who also visits frequently. 'You see that woman,' he once said, sighing and pointing at his mom, 'from her hands even coffee was food.' I understood perfectly what he was saying.

Romanian Eggplant Salad with Figs & Antipasto

Mama's signature dish

ROMANIAN EGGPLANT SALAD
4 medium eggplants
1 clove garlic
1 onion, chopped roughly
salt and freshly ground pepper, to taste
½ cup olive oil

Pierce eggplants in several places with a fork. Grill directly over gas flame on all sides until eggplants collapse and flesh begins to soften. Remove from heat, allow to cool and bitter juices to drain off. Scoop out cooked flesh. Blend eggplant, garlic, onion, salt, pepper and olive oil until very smooth.

ANTIPASTO
6 large fresh figs, halved
rocket
artichokes
baby Roma tomatoes
black olives
marinated feta cheese
shaved parmesan cheese
3 teaspoons balsamic vinegar
pita chips or slices of fresh crusty bread

Place eggplant salad in large ramekin on the side of a serving platter. Arrange figs, feta and other vegetables next to the dip. Sprinkle vegetables with parmesan and drizzle with balsamic vinegar. Serve with pita chips or slices of fresh crusty bread.
(SERVES 6)

BASIL HIRSCHOWITZ

Basil Hirschowitz is a gastroenterologist and academic, best known for inventing the first flexible fibreoptic endoscope in 1956.

He was born in 1925 in Bethal, South Africa, the son of Morris and Dorothy.

Being a talented student, Basil completed his first degree in his teens at the University of the Witwatersrand, furthered his studies in the UK and earned an MD degree in 1954 from the University of the Witwatersrand. He moved to the United States, settling in Birmingham, Alabama. He has held many positions including professor of medicine and professor of physiology and biophysics at the University of Alabama, culminating in professor emeritus of medicine.

The fibreoptic endoscope revolutionised this field of medicine and led to optical fibre communication in multiple industries. Basil's original invention is now in the Smithsonian Institution in Washington, DC.

Basil has been a visiting professor at universities in the US and England, has presided over numerous boards and committees, and has authored over 300 published papers. He has been honoured with many awards in the field of the healing arts, including the Schindler Medal from the American Society for Gastrointestinal Endoscopy, the Charles F. Kettering Prize from the General Motors Cancer Research Foundation, is an honorary fellow of the Royal Society of Medicine, and has an honorary MD from Gothenburg University in Sweden.

Basil is married to Barbara and they have two sons, two daughters and five grandchildren.

Food From 'the Old Country'

An invitation to recall one's childhood memories is a challenge few can resist. A kaleidoscope of images instantly appears through the fuzzy lens of time. My earliest food memory, at age four or five, is the fragrance of bread baking in my grandmother, Bobbe Zlate's, kitchen. With a shiver of anticipation, I would watch her slice the loaf as she held it against her chest.

Living as I do in Alabama, there are many dishes I haven't eaten in years, nostalgic foods of my European-born parents' immigrant generation. The cornucopia of products from my mother's kitchen in Bethal, a small farming town 120 km east of Johannesburg, could take up a whole book and still be incomplete. A sampler will have to do.

I deeply miss the *kichel*, a delicate baked shell, curled up at the edges and coated on one side with sugar. After being rolled out very thinly, the *kichel* dough would be placed on a wooden paddle, similar to one used in a pizzeria, and slid into a very hot Aga oven for a few seconds until golden and curled. These formed the indispensable perfect container for holding and eating *gehakte* (chopped) herring to give an explosion of sweet and sour and salty. *Kichel* was also savoured with that other specialty, chopped liver, made with real chicken *schmaltz* (fat) and, to borrow from Admiral Farragut,[1] damn the coronaries, full steam ahead!

Fresh fish on ice arrived by rail on Fridays. This would be used to create our traditional Shabbat *gefilte* fish, little balls of minced fish mixed with eggs, onion and spices and boiled with carrots and onions. We would eat this delicacy with freshly grated *chrain* (horseradish) or special sweet mustard, accompanied by the Shabbat *challah* to sop up the gravy. The present bottled variety doesn't even vaguely resemble that wonderful mainstay of the Friday night supper.

It was traditional for a Jewish family to cook at least one chicken in honour of the Shabbat. The aroma of the traditional therapeutic chicken soup with *lokshen* or noodles, handmade from scratch that day, permeated our home each week. Every part of the chicken was used and dishes such as *pupiks* (roasted gizzards), chopped liver, *helzel* (stuffed chicken neck), *schmaltz* (fat) and *grebenis* (chicken skins fried with chopped onions in chicken fat) were created.

Smoked mutton chops bought at Crystal's, a well-known kosher delicatessen in Doornfontein, the predominantly Jewish 'East End' of Johannesburg, formed the basis of many interesting dishes; one of my favourites was a heavenly stew cooked with potatoes.

---

1   Admiral David Glasgow Farragut was the US senior naval officer during the American Civil War. He is remembered for his famous order at the Battle of Mobile Bay, 'Damn the torpedoes, full speed ahead!'

My earliest food memory, at age four or five, is the fragrance of bread baking in my grandmother, Bobbe Zlate's, kitchen. With a shiver of anxiety, I would watch her slice the loaf as she held it against her chest.

Hirschowitz family circa 1928 – Basil *(seated, front row, fourth from right)*, his grandmother Zlate *(seated, second row, third from right)*, his father Morris *(seated, second row, first from right)*, his mother Dolly *(standing, third row, second from right)*.

My mother Dorothy was affectionately known as Auntie Dolly but her grandchildren called her Tally. To me, her baking surpassed anyone's in the family and my daughters still drool when they talk of Tally's chocolate cake. I long for her traditional *yom tov* (holiday) sweets – her *nashe teiglach*, the small knotted pastries boiled in honeyed syrup and often filled with nuts (dare one call them wet profiteroles?); *pletzlach*, minced dried apricot candies; and *bulkes*, cinnamon yeast buns. Her bagels, boiled before baking as any good bagel should be, were superb.

Blending the old country, Lithuania, with the new, we eagerly adopted a traditional South African food called *biltong*, beef cut into thick strips and heavily spiced and air-dried. I recall this delicacy with almost physical longing. *Biltong* was a specialty from Moolenbeek's butchery, a business located in Market Street and a block away from Bethal shul. We would eat the *biltong* on its own or sliced thin with a sharp pocket knife or accompanied with black bread spread with chicken *schmaltz* and finely chopped sweet onions. I have tried to make *biltong* here in Alabama, but it has never turned out the same.

And so, in distant exiles our taste-buds carry the tender, savoury nostalgic memories of time and cultures past, but not forgotten.

Kichel

A little treasure handed down from my mother

8 eggs

pinch salt

¼ teaspoon ground ginger

½ cup vegetable oil

2½–3 cups plain flour, sifted

extra plain flour, for rolling

extra oil, for brushing

white sugar, for coating shells

Preheat oven to 200°C. Cover cooling racks with aluminum foil or baking paper; this will give the *kichel* a wavy look during baking process.

Separate eggs, placing 8 yolks in one bowl and 4 whites in another. Beat egg yolks until thick, add salt, ginger and oil. Beat egg whites until stiff. Using electric mixer on low speed, fold whites into the yolks until just lightly mixed. Add enough flour to form sticky dough.

Lightly flour a flat surface or board. Roll out dough in small batches until very thin. The dough is very sticky and extra flour may be needed. Evenly prick the pastry all over with a fork and brush lightly with oil using a pastry brush. Cut into shapes such as diamonds, squares or into circles using a round cookie-cutter.

Place extra sugar into a bowl and dip the oiled side of the pastry into sugar. Place pastry shapes, sugar side up, on prepared cooling racks and bake for about 4–5 minutes in the hot oven until just golden. Cool completely and store in airtight containers.

Beware: The *kichel* bake extremely quickly and **must be watched** to prevent burning.

(MAKES ABOUT 50 PIECES)

LORD JANNER
OF BRAUNSTONE

Lord Greville Janner of Braunstone QC is a retired Labour member of the House of Lords.

He was born in 1928 in Cardiff, Wales, the son of Sir Barnett and Lady Elsie Janner.

After evacuating to Canada during World War II, Lord Janner went to Bishop's College School in Lennoxville, Quebec. Later graduating from Trinity Hall, Cambridge, he received a Fulbright and Smith-Mundt scholarship to Harvard Law School and in 1954 became a barrister.

Lord Janner was appointed a QC (Queens Counsel) in 1971. He represented Leicester North West and then Leicester West in the House of Commons from 1970 until his retirement in 1997. His predecessor in the seat was his father. Greville Janner was raised to the life peerage as Lord Janner of Braunstone for Leicester in the County of Leicestershire in 1997.

Lord Janner was president of the Board of Deputies of British Jews from 1978–84, and a key international figure in efforts to seek reparations for Holocaust victims. He was instrumental in arranging the 1997 London Nazi Looted Gold conference. He was chair of the Parliamentary Select Committee on Employment from 1994–96. Lord Janner is founder and president of the Commonwealth Jewish Council and chairman of the Holocaust Educational Trust.

Throughout his career, Lord Janner has sought to foster good relations between different faiths and religions. His book *One Hand Alone Cannot Clap* is testament to this work. He is a member of the Magic Circle and the International Brotherhood of Magicians.

Lord Janner is gifted in linguistics and can speak nine languages. His other interests include autograph collections, glass and other artefacts, swimming, and above all, his family. In 1955 he married Australian Myra Sheink, who passed away in 1996. He has three children and many grandchildren.

Joint Zuteilungen

As an eighteen-year-old serviceman in the British army of the Rhine, I was taken to the site of the former concentration camp of Bergen-Belsen on the second anniversary of its liberation. The SS army barracks nearby had become the only Jewish Displaced Persons camp in the British zone of Germany. There, its inmates held a service of remembrance by the mass graves. It tore me apart.

At the end of the service when we had all said *Kaddish* (a prayer cited by mourners), I was taken for tea to the small single-storey building that had become the Jewish orphanage, the *Kinderheim*.

The children were dressed in uniforms made from American army blankets. I joined them for supper – the most memorable meal of my life. The food was grim: dry brown bread, inedible gruel and tea or juice. The lad beside me taught me my first word of Yiddish: "*Ess,*" he commanded. Eat, Gabriel. Then we played ping-pong and they adopted me as their *Englischherzlner*. Every Friday night, I hitched to Belsen and joined them for their Shabbat meal.

Then I moved into the camp and made friends with the people and was invited to their homes. The key to their survival was weekly packets provided by the American Joint Distribution Committee, known as *Joint Zuteilungen*.

Some of the displaced persons (the Jewish DPs) set up stalls in the streets and sold food, clothing and other essentials for survival. And if you did not want your parcel from the *Joint*, they would buy it from you and sell it on.

Enraged by the miseries of these people, I became the youngest war crimes investigator in the British army. I spent the next eighteen months hunting down criminals who had not only run concentration camps and murdered Jews and others in the villages and homes, but who had starved prisoners to death. Yes, food is an essential of life – and the *Joint Zuteilungen* became for me the symbols of survival.

Fresh Blood-Orange Marmalade
A simple pleasure — bread and jam

1¼ cups thinly sliced, seeded blood
  oranges, from 2–3 oranges

1¼ cups water
2¼ cups jam-setting sugar

Place oranges and water in a saucepan. Bring to the boil and cook rapidly for 20 minutes or until tender. Add sugar, reduce heat to low and stir until the sugar dissolves. Increase heat and again boil rapidly for about 40 minutes, until the bubbling stops and the oranges become opaque. Whilst cooling, skim the foam off the surface and stir thoroughly. Store in refrigerator for 4–5 days.

(MAKES 2 CUPS)

Pear & Ginger Jam

2½ cups pears, peeled, cored and diced
  small, from 4–5 pears
¼ cup preserved ginger, cut into
  small chunks

2½ cups jam-setting sugar
½ cup water
2cm piece fresh ginger, peeled
1 lemon, juiced

Place all ingredients into a saucepan and stir over a gentle heat until sugar has dissolved. Increase heat and boil rapidly, stirring occasionally, until very thick. Remove ginger. Using a slotted spoon, divide and place the fruit into sterilised jars. Pour remaining syrup evenly over the fruit. Seal and cool. Store in refrigerator for 4–5 days.

(MAKES 2½ CUPS)

Barbara Kirshenblatt-Gimblett is a university professor and professor of performance studies at New York University.

BARBARA KIRSHENBLATT-GIMBLETT

She was born in Toronto, Canada, the daughter of Mayer and Doris Kirshenblatt. Her parents had emigrated from Poland before the Second World War.

Barbara majored in English at the University of Toronto, and in 1965 moved to the US where she studied at the University of California, Berkeley, and received her PhD in folklore from Indiana University. After teaching at the University of Texas and the University of Pennsylvania, Barbara was asked to chair the department of performance studies at NYU's Tisch School of the Arts. Barbara is also affiliated professor of Hebrew and Judaic studies. She lectures on a variety of subjects including Jewish culture, museums and food.

Barbara has received many awards and prizes, notably the Guggenheim Fellowship. The Melton Center for Jewish Studies at Ohio State University honoured Barbara as Distinguished Humanist for 2003. She is the author of many books including *Image Before My Eyes: A Photographic History of Jewish Life in Poland, 1864–1939* (with Lucjan Dobroszycki) and *Destination Culture: Tourism, Museum and Heritage*. More recently, Barbara collaborated with her father Mayer on *They Called Me Mayer July: Painted Memories of a Jewish Childhood in Poland Before the Holocaust*.

Barbara has always had a passion for gathering printed material. In college she began collecting books and has built up her own personal library which houses one of the largest collections of Jewish cookbooks in the world. Her cookbooks cover every conceivable cuisine and specialised subject associated with food – from salt, sourdough, tropical fruit, cod, New York State apples and edible insects to napkin-folding. Many of these books not only satisfy her curiosity but provide the basis for her teaching and writing on food.

Barbara and her husband Max, an artist, live in New York.

The Soup Pot Never Left the Stove

Barbara's father Mayer made it his mission to remember the world of his childhood in Poland in living colour. Barbara has been interviewing her father for forty years; after much encouragement, in 1990 at the age of 73, he began to paint what he could remember. These interviews and paintings are the basis for They Called Me Mayer July: Painted Memories of a Jewish Childhood in Poland Before the Holocaust.

'We had a wood burning stove in the corner of the kitchen. The brick sides of the stove were covered with clay to seal the surface and then whitewashed. This is the same technique they used on the exterior walls of buildings. Along the narrow side of the stove were two doors to the fire. We put the wood into the stove through the larger door. The wood rested on a steel grate. The ashes would fall through the grate and we would remove them through the smaller door. We could control the fire by opening or closing the little door to the ashes. The more air we let in, the more quickly and hot the fire would burn. The baking oven was a metal box inside the brick stove. It was surrounded by the fire. The door to the baking oven was on the wide side of the stove. It had a latch handle. When the fire died down, the bricks and metal retained heat. In winter, mother baked in her own oven. In summer, it was too hot to bake at home so mother took her *challahs* and cakes to the baker's oven.

The surface of the stove consisted of a large metal plate. Four holes in the metal plate served as burners. Each burner was covered with three or four concentric rings. You could control the heat by adding or removing rings. Mother would remove all the rings from one of the burners to expose the hot coals when she was making a *meygl*. To make a *meygl* she would clean the skin of the chicken neck as best she could, fill the skin with flour and chicken fat, season it with salt and pepper, and sew up the ends. Then she would put the *meygl* on the hot coals for a few seconds to expand the air inside the skin and make it inflate. The fire would also singe the fine feather fuzz and make it easier for her to scrape the skin clean. She would then place the *meygl* in a pan and roast it with the chicken in the oven. The stuffing would expand and the skin would stay inflated and become crisp. This was a great delicacy.

The teakettle and soup pot never left the stove. When mother was ready to cook, she would light the fire. The hottest heat was under the front two burners. She would set the soup pot on one of the back burners so that it would cook slowly. One never knew what scrap would be found throughout the day, a carrot, a potato, barley, a piece of chicken, or even a piece of meat. By the end of the day there was soup. You didn't even wash out the soup pot, because a little bit of flavour remained in the pot. Even now, I feel that a day without soup is not a day.'

Dora's Leek, Barley & Split Pea Soup

Remember Dora, Barbara's mother, every time you serve this delicious hearty soup – a staple and elixir during cold winters in eastern Poland

3 large leeks with dark green tops, washed

2 large carrots, diced

1 large parsnip, diced

6 celery stalks and leaves, diced

2½ cups split green peas, washed

⅔ cup whole barley, washed and soaked

½ cup large white lima beans, soaked

salt and freshly ground black pepper

dill, chopped coarsely

flat-leaf parsley, chopped coarsely

Make stock: Bring 8 cups of water to the boil in a large pot. Cut off the dark green tops of leeks and set aside. Thinly slice the white part of the leeks and set aside. Place leek tops into the boiling water, reduce heat and simmer until very soft. Using a slotted spoon, remove and discard the tops and add white part of the leeks, carrots, parsnip and celery to the pot. Bring back to the boil and simmer until vegetables are cooked. Add salt and pepper to taste.

Make soup: In a separate pot, combine split peas with 4 cups of water. Bring to the boil, reduce heat and simmer until soft, about 40 minutes. Process until smooth and stir through the stock and vegetables. Add barley and lima beans to the pot and simmer until soft, about 40 minutes. Add extra water for desired consistency. Serve garnished with dill and parsley.

Note: Soup freezes well.

(SERVES 10–12)

With delis, gourmet food shops and
countless restaurants and cafes,
New York is a mecca for food lovers.

MARC SALEM

Marc Salem is an academic, entertainer and a world authority on non-verbal communication.

He was born Moshe Botwinick in 1953 in Philadelphia, the son of a rabbi and a pharmacist. Salem is his wife's maiden name.

Marc holds degrees in psychology and cognitive science. As a student of the human mind for over thirty years, he has lectured in major universities, focusing on how the mind creates reality.

Marc was a director of research at the Children's Television Workshop, the producers of *Sesame Street,* where he helped create this educational show. His expertise has also assisted law firms and law enforcement cases.

His show *Mind Games*, where he uses his academic training and gift for reading people's minds, became a theatre fixture in 1997 and has had sell-out performances around the world. Marc has been featured on television and radio and is the author of *The Six Keys to Unlock and Empower Your Mind*.

Marc is married to Tova and lives in New York City. He has three sons and four grandsons.

Celebrating the Paradox

I spend up to eight months of the year travelling, performing my show *Mind Games*. As someone who keeps kosher, the dietary restrictions are difficult. Some countries and cities are easier than others. Edinburgh boasts one of the world's best vegetarian restaurants, where they serve a vegetarian haggis. A bit of an oxymoron, no? Yet rather than sheep's offal minced with onions, flour, fats and spices boiled in the animal's stomach, this version is made of cabbage, garlic, leeks and soy served with a red pepper sauce.

Our language is littered with oxymorons, especially when it comes to food: *wickedly good, bitter-sweet, diet ice-cream, evaporated milk, fat-free cream cheese, fresh-frozen, fresh sour cream, healthy white chocolate, kosher bacon bits, non-alcoholic beer/wine, non-dairy creamer, sweet 'n' sour, vegetarian meatballs.*

I have delightful childhood memories of our festivals; indeed, they remain special times for family, friends and good food. Yet these occasions are full of paradoxes. *Rosh Hashanah* is a celebration: the sweetness of a new year, new clothes and special foods; yet it is also a Day of Judgement: 'Who will live and who will die?' On *Purim*, where we remember Haman's failed plot to annihilate our people, we eat the tasty *hamantashen* (three-cornered pastry filled with nuts, jam or poppy seeds representing the hat of the evil Haman); and on *Chanukah*, the Festival of Lights, we eat fried potato *latkes* and sweet jelly-jam doughnuts. On another level, the paradox here is that on *Purim* the enemy physically attacked the Jewish people and they responded spiritually by praying, while on *Chanukah* the Greeks attacked the Jewish people spiritually by desecrating the Temple and the Jews responded physically.

Yet the greatest paradoxes are evident during Passover, where we remember slavery and celebrate freedom. We sit around the table for the *Seder,* reading and singing songs in a specific order about the Exodus from Egypt, remembering our freedom while recalling the bitterness of our years as slaves under the cruel rule of the pharaohs. We recline on cushions like royalty to show we are free. Yet we dip our food in salt water to remind us of the tears of slavery, and eat *maror* (horseradish) to remember the bitter times. We drink four cups of wine to represent our liberation but we eat *charoset* (a sweet mixture of crushed nuts, wine, cinnamon and apples) to commemorate the mortar bricks we were forced to make. Usually bread is served at a meal. However, throughout this feast, we eat unleavened bread called *matzo*. This culinary experience is steeped in long-held traditions and symbolism.

Which brings me to the ultimate paradox of our *Seder*: my mother's Passover bagel. This quintessential Jewish bread is usually made from yeasted wheat dough. Yet despite Passover being a time of no bread, my mother still managed to put a bagel on the table. Indeed, the mention of 'Passover bagel' brings a smile to my face.

Passover Bagels

A Salem family favourite to share

1 cup cold water
½ cup vegetable oil
1 cup *matzo* meal *

½ cup matzo cake flour
¼ cup white sugar
5 large eggs

Preheat oven to 180°C. Combine water and oil in a saucepan and bring to the boil. Remove from the heat. Using a wooden spoon, stir in the *matzo* meal, flour and sugar. Add one egg at a time to the mixture, beating until well-blended. Grease or line a baking tray with baking paper. Place heaped tablespoons of the dough evenly across sheet. Dip your finger in cold water and make a hole in the centre of each to make a bagel. Bake for 30 minutes or until golden. Best eaten on the day of baking.

  * *Matzo* is the unleavened bread made without yeast or any other raising agent and eaten during the eight-day festival of Passover. This celebration commemorates the exodus of the Israelites from captivity in Egypt.

(MAKES 18 SMALL BAGELS)

Fresh Tomato Soup

1½ kg fresh ripe tomatoes, roughly
    chopped
1 cup water
salt and freshly ground black pepper,
    to taste

fresh basil, flat-leaf parsley or chives,
    finely chopped

Place tomatoes, water, salt and pepper into a saucepan and bring to the boil. Reduce heat, cover and simmer for 10 minutes. Blend the soup until smooth. Push the soup through a fine sieve to remove tomato seeds and skins. If the soup is too thick, add extra water to bring to the desired consistency. Reheat when ready to serve. Garnish with chopped herbs.

  Note: A thicker version makes a wonderful sauce for pasta, fish, chicken and meat.

(SERVES 6)

ART SPIEGELMAN

Art Spiegelman is an American cartoonist and editor, best known for his Pulitzer Prize-winning comic *Maus*.

KAPUSNIAK- 6-8 servings
- 1 pound of sauerkraut, canned or fresh, the more sour the better.
- 2 pounds Flanken, or short ribs.
- ½ cup brown sugar.
- 2 crushed cloves of garlic
- 1 pound canned tomatoes
- 4 cups of water

Place everything into a 5 quart kettle and simmer for 2-2½ hours, stirring frequently, until the meat is tender. Remove meat, then skim fat off soup. (If possible, refrigerate overnight, then remove congealed fat.)
Cut meat into bite-size pieces and replace into soup. Reheat and serve.

Once I invited my High School pal, Jon Wong, for some of Mom's home-cooking. It was February and she served up my favorite winter dish, a hot, steamy, tangy

KAPUSNIAK

a soup recipe from the Old Country that makes those Campbells Hearty "Man-Pleasers" seem like limp-wristed sissy-water by comparison.

Jon looked dubiously at the savory bowl and gingerly tried a tentative half-spoonful of the indescribable sweet-and-sour broth. His mouth puckered to a tiny asterisk as if he'd swallowed a live frog. For five minutes he made soft, quick panting sounds while the Spiegelman family happily slurped through several helpings. Jon finally found his voice and hoarsely whispered: "I can't believe it – Jews eat SAUERKRAUT soup!"

He refused to try another drop, or even try the CHULENT stew that Mom made as the main dish... I guess he thought it was made with dead babies.

ONCE I invited my High School pal, Jon Wong, for some of Mom's home-cooking!

DONNA JACOBS-SIFE

Donna Jacobs-Sife is a singer/songwriter, storyteller and peace worker.

She was born in 1956 in Sydney, Australia. Her parents Lesley and Lionel migrated from Scotland and New Zealand. Her maternal grandmother Leah Josephs came from Riga, Latvia.

Donna volunteered to teach Jewish studies when her children started school and more than twenty years later continues to teach. Her career as a professional storyteller stems from her teaching and her Judaism. Social themes of peace, non-violence and conflict resolution with an underlying message of common decency form the basis of her storytelling and performances.

Donna has travelled around Australia, the USA, the UK and Israel, teaching, singing and storytelling. She has performed at many festivals, conferences, celebrations, religious and academic institutions. Recognised as a peace activist, Donna has been invited to reconciliation events and inter-religious gatherings, and has been involved in workshops for Christian, Baha'i and Muslim teachers.

Her story 'The Wall' won first place at the Australian National Storytelling Festival in 1997. She contributes to the *Australian Jewish News* and other journals. Her CD *Living in Harmony*, produced with renowned musician Llew Kiek, is a collaboration of stories dealing with society's growing tensions.

Donna has three children and lives in Sydney.

Soul Food

I have vivid childhood memories of our Passover *Seder* at my aunt's house. I remember the long table taking up the whole room, making it a major achievement to seat the whole family. Only those sitting on the ends could get up to help serve the plates of roast chicken, *matzo* ball soup, sweet and sour beans, baked vegetable dishes, potato *kugel* and *tzimmes*. Soul food. Remnants of a bygone world.

This room had a small frosted window that always remained ajar. While the others sang of freedom, I, being the dreamer of the family, would stare out that window and imagine Jews everywhere doing the same thing – a thought that gave me great comfort. I come from the non-believing, non-kosher side of the family. These moments made me aware of something greater, something beyond.

When I became a mother, I wanted to recreate those soul food moments for my children. One year, just before *Rosh Hashanah*, I started to remember the taste of my auntie's *tzimmes*. So I went to buy carrots and prunes, came home and experimented. The first attempt was too dry. The next not sweet enough, not thick enough. There was a particular quality I was aiming for.

During one attempt I turned the oven to very low, forgot about it and went to bed. When I woke in the morning the smell in the house evoked something very powerful in my memory. It was the quality I could not describe, but knew had been missing. The result was a rich and thick dish, dark in colour, and heavy with meaning.

But this is not the end of the story. A couple of years after the great *tzimmes* discovery, I visited my auntie after Passover. She had some leftover *tzimmes* in the fridge and asked if I wanted some. Of course I did. But the taste was nothing like I remembered. 'Is this the same *tzimmes* you served at *Seder* when I was little?' She insisted she had not changed the recipe for forty years.

We agreed to meet the following week so she could taste some of my *tzimmes*. I wanted to remind her that long ago, she really did make a different *tzimmes*. We sat down together and I watched as she raised the fork to her lips and chewed ponderously. To my astonishment, her eyes filled with tears. Leaning forward, she put her hand on my arm and said, 'Donna-le, this is the *tzimmes* my mother used to make.'

My grandmother died when I was five. Somehow it was that taste, that quality I remembered, that had been so hard to reproduce. Soul food. What else would you call it?

Carrot Tzimmes Soufflé

Tzimmes means 'big fuss' or a complicated situation in Yiddish. This is a sweet melange of cooked carrots, prunes, honey and brown sugar, seasoned with cinnamon; it is a traditional accompaniment to Jewish holiday meals.

SOUFFLÉ

1–2 tablespoons dry breadcrumbs

¼ cup plain flour

1 cup milk

¼ cup butter

1 cup tasty cheese, finely grated

¼ teaspoon white pepper

6 egg yolks, lightly beaten

1½ cups carrot *tzimmes*

6 egg whites

¼ teaspoon cream of tartar

CARROT *TZIMMES*

4 large carrots, peeled and roughly sliced

1 small potato, peeled and cubed

1 small kumara or orange sweet potato, peeled and cubed

½ medium brown onion, diced

5 prunes, pitted and halved

½ small clove garlic, crushed

1 tablespoon brown sugar

½ teaspoon salt

½ teaspoon ground cinnamon, optional

½ cup orange juice

Make tzimmes: Place all ingredients in a saucepan and bring to the boil. Reduce heat, simmer and stir occasionally, until the vegetables are very soft but not mushy. If the liquid has boiled away, add a little water. Blend until smooth. Reserve 1½ cups *tzimmes* for the soufflé.

Prepare soufflé dish: Butter a 6-cup (1½ litre) soufflé dish. Make a collar by measuring enough foil to go around the dish one and a half times. Fold the foil in half lengthwise and tie it around the rim. The collar should extend at least 5cm above the rim. Coat bottom and sides of dish with breadcrumbs.

Make soufflé: Preheat oven to 180°C. Combine flour and milk, ensuring all lumps dissolve. Melt butter in a saucepan over low heat and add flour and milk. Stir and cook for about 5 minutes, until it thickens. Remove from heat and add cheese, white pepper, stirring until smooth. Add egg yolks, two tablespoons at a time, mixing well. Stir in *tzimmes* and set aside. Beat egg whites with cream of tartar until stiff. Gently fold *tzimmes* mixture through the whites. Spoon mixture into the prepared soufflé dish. Run a knife across the top to ensure soufflé surface is flat. To ensure soufflé rises upright, run a finger around the inner rim of the dish. Bake for 30 minutes or until golden brown, puffy and almost set. Remove the collar and serve immediately.

* The remainder can be used as a side dish or with a main course.

Note: 6 individual 1-cup ramekins can be prepared in the same manner.

(SERVES 4–6)

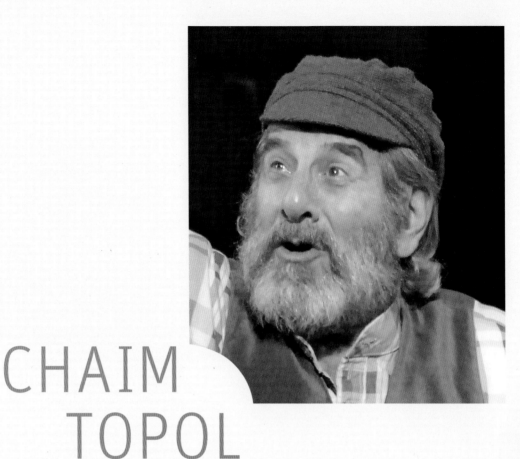

CHAIM TOPOL

Chaim Topol, one of Israel's most famous actors, was born in 1935 in Tel Aviv.

He is best known for his performance in *Fiddler on the Roof* in the role of Tevye, the milkman.

Chaim's acting career began during his army service when he joined Lahakat Hanahal, a unit that toured the country entertaining troops. He returned to his kibbutz after leaving the army.

He founded a travelling satirical theatre, Batzal Yarok, and went on to act with the Haifa Theatre. His film debut, a comedy *I Like Mike*, and his award-winning performance in the film *Sallah* led him to play Tevye in the 1967 London stage production of *Fiddler on the Roof*. Following the 1971 Norman Jewison film release of *Fiddler*, Chaim received a Golden Globe Award and also an Academy Award nomination in 1972.

Chaim has acted in many films including *Before Winter Comes*, *A Talent for Loving*, *The Public Eye*, *Galileo*, *The House on Garibaldi Street*, *Flash Gordon*, the James Bond movie *For Your Eyes Only*, *The Winds of War*, *War and Remembrance*, *Queenie* and *A Dime Novel*. He has acted in many theatre productions and continues to perform as Tevye in *Fiddler on the Roof*, always receiving rave reviews.

Chaim has written two books, *Topol by Topol* and *To Life! A Treasury of Jewish Wisdom, Wit and Humour*, and has illustrated 25.

Chaim is married to Galia and they have three children.

Funny Men and Their Food

*T*eddy Kollek and I had a close friend in common and, whenever I got an urgent summons to the mayor's office, I could be fairly certain that Danny Kaye was in town. Danny was one of the most versatile people I knew. He was a splendid cook and an expert on Chinese cuisine. When I stayed in his Beverly Hills home for a week, he provided twelve-course Chinese meals every night without serving the same course twice. Danny had a special stove for his Chinese cooking, with all the condiments stacked in neat racks around him and to watch him prepare the meal was like watching a ballet as he danced from rack to stove and from stove to rack picking up a jar here, a jar there. I once suggested going to a Chinese restaurant in the Jewish-populated suburb of Golders Green for dinner. Danny went along with us. We ordered one dish and Danny thought he recognised the hand of the chef. He then asked for a dish of chicken cubes with chestnuts, and when he took one bite, he rose from the table and turned into the kitchen. When I went in after him I found him embracing the chef like a long lost brother. 'I told you I recognised him,' he said. 'He's from the Princess Gardens restaurant in Hong Kong.'

~

One stormy night, Monty Bloom, soaked to the skin, ran into the delicatessen.

'A smoked salmon bagel and a salt beef sandwich please,' said Monty to the man behind the counter. 'Oh, and some of your strudel, cheesecake and *lockshen* pudding.'

'Is that all?' asked the assistant.

'Yes, I think that's all she wanted,' said Monty, his teeth chattering.

'For your wife is it?'

'My wife? Of course it's for my wife! Do you think my *mother* would send me out on a night like this?'

~

A rabbi and a priest were having breakfast. The priest ordered bacon and eggs and turned to the rabbi: 'Rabbi, when are you going to start enjoying some of this delicious bacon?'

'At your wedding!' replied the rabbi.

Adapted from Chaim Topol's Topol by Topol *(Weidenfeld and Nicolson, 1981) and* To Life! A Treasury of Wit and Humour *(Robson Books, 1994) used with permission of Chaim Topol.*

Fish Quenelles with Two Sauces
The Fiddler's favourite

These poached balls of minced fish are also known as gefilte fish.

QUENELLE MIXTURE
2 tablespoons oil
2 tablespoons margarine or butter
3 white onions, finely sliced
2kg white fish fillets, minced (fishmonger will do this for you)
4 tablespoons fine *matzo* meal or breadcrumbs
3 eggs
3 teaspoons salt
2 teaspoons white sugar
½ teaspoon white pepper
1 cup iced water

POACHING BROTH
3 white onions
2 carrots, peeled and sliced into rounds
12 cups water
1 teaspoon salt
1 teaspoon sugar
½ teaspoon white pepper

DILL SAUCE
3 cups whole egg mayonnaise
3 cups fresh dill, very finely chopped
1–2 tablespoons lemon juice
white pepper and salt, to taste

RED PEPPER SAUCE
3 cups whole egg mayonnaise
10 strips pickled red peppers/capsicums
1 teaspoon prepared white horseradish

Make quenelles: Heat oil and margarine and fry onions until just soft. Gently combine remaining fish quenelle ingredients in a large bowl, mixing thoroughly. Add more iced water if the mixture is too stiff. Using slightly moistened hands, shape into 3–4cm round or oval-shaped quenelles and refrigerate until firm.

Make poaching broth: Place all ingredients in a large pot and bring to the boil, reduce heat and simmer for 15 minutes. Bring poaching broth back to the boil, drop in the quenelles and reduce heat. Simmer covered for 1 hour, gently stirring occasionally to ensure quenelles do not stick to the bottom. Remove pot from heat. Allow to cool to room temperature. Remove quenelles with a slotted spoon and place them in a dish. Strain the broth through a fine sieve, pour over the quenelles and refrigerate until ready to use.

Make dill sauce: Blend all ingredients. *Make red pepper sauce:* Blend all ingredients. Place two quenelles onto individual serving plates. Pour dill sauce over one and red pepper sauce over the other, so that they are both well coated.
(SERVES 12)

above: Chaim Topol as Tevye the milkman in 'Fiddler on the Roof'.

above right: Barbara Kirshenblatt-Gimblatt with her father, Mayer.

below left: Lord Janner as a child.

below right: George Dreyfus's parents, Hilde and Alfred; a musical score by George Dreyfus.

© Copyright MCMLXXV by Allans Music Australia Ltd. Melbourne

Notenbeispiel 2: George Dreyfus, Filmmusik zu «Rush» (1974), Partiturseite 1 (T. 1–4) in der Handschrift des Komponisten.

left: Mayer Kirshenblatt's painting 'The Soup Pot Never Left the Stove'.

below: Tovah Feldshuh as Golda Meir.

Asparagus Teriyaki

500g or 3 bunches green asparagus, washed and trimmed

DRESSING
⅓ cup olive oil
⅓ cup low salt soy sauce
¼ cup sugar
1 tablespoon white sesame seeds

Make dressing: Place all ingredients in a screw-top jar and shake well.

Place asparagus in pot of boiling water and cook for 3 minutes, or microwave until just tender and still bright green. Drain and plunge in ice-cold water to stop cooking process. Drain asparagus on paper towel and place on a platter. Pour over dressing and serve.

Note: French beans can be used in place of asparagus.

(SERVES 4–5)

~

Chicken & Corn Soup

2 teaspoons sesame oil
2 spring onions, thinly sliced
1 clove garlic, crushed
4 cups water
4 cups chicken stock, fresh or made using 4 stock cubes dissolved in 4 cups boiling water
200g chicken breasts, finely sliced or use skinned BBQ chicken breast

1 x 310g can corn kernels
1 x 310g can creamed corn
1 tablespoon cornflour, blended with ¼ cup water
1 egg, lightly beaten
salt and freshly ground black pepper, to taste
extra spring onions, finely sliced for garnish

Heat sesame oil in a large saucepan, gently fry onions and garlic until soft. Add water and chicken stock and bring to the boil. Reduce heat, add chicken and simmer for a few minutes until chicken is cooked. Add corn kernels, creamed corn, blended cornflour, salt and pepper. Stir constantly until the soup boils and thickens slightly. Just before serving, slowly pour egg in a thin stream into soup and stir through very gently to form *ribbons*. Serve in bowls and garnish.

(SERVES 4)

Brie En Cocotte: Baked Brie in Puff Pastry

1 sheet frozen puff pastry, thawed at
    room temperature
plain flour

½ cup chives, finely sliced
1 x 500g round brie cheese*
1 egg yolk mixed with 1 teaspoon water

Preheat oven to 200°C. Line a baking tray with baking paper.

Lightly flour a clean flat surface and lay out puff pastry. Sprinkle chives over puff pastry and roll out thinly. Wrap dough around brie. Trim and reserve excess pastry. Press edges of pastry with your fingers to seal. Place on baking tray, seam-side down. Cut decorative shapes, such as leaves, from excess pastry and place on brie. Brush with egg wash and bake for 15 to 20 minutes until golden. Remove from oven and allow to rest for about 20 minutes before serving. Serve baked brie whole or sliced on individual plates.

*Brie is a soft, ripened cheese with a white rind made from cows' milk with a delicate taste and smooth texture. It was created in the 7th century in France. Brie is best served at room temperature.

(SERVES 6)

~

Lentil Soup with Garlic & Cumin

1 cup dried red lentils
1 x 400g tin whole peeled tomatoes
3 vegetable stock cubes dissolved in
    2 cups of water
2 large cloves garlic, crushed

1 large onion, peeled and chopped
2 teaspoons ground cumin
1 teaspoon salt
freshly ground black pepper, to taste
30g butter or margarine

Make soup: Wash lentils in a strainer and remove any hard stones. Drain tinned tomatoes and reserve juice. Place lentils, stock, 3 whole tomatoes, tomato juice, garlic and half the onion into a saucepan and bring to the boil. Reduce heat and simmer for 30 minutes. Add cumin, salt and pepper and process in a blender until smooth. Add extra water if a thinner consistency is desired.

Make garnish: Melt butter in a non-stick pan and fry remaining onion until golden and crispy.

Serve soup garnished with fried onion.

(SERVES 4–6)

Chicken Consommé with Pesto Chicken Dumplings

350g lean chicken breast mince
½ cup breadcrumbs
2 tablespoons pesto or 2 tablespoons
   fresh basil, finely chopped
2 cloves garlic, crushed
salt and freshly ground pepper, to taste
1 teaspoon olive oil
1 long red chilli, seeded and thinly
   sliced

4 cups clear chicken soup, fresh or made
   using 4 stock cubes dissolved in 4
   cups boiling water
2 cups baby spinach leaves, finely
   shredded
1 red capsicum, sliced into julienne strips

Make dumplings: Combine chicken mince, breadcrumbs, pesto, garlic, salt and pepper in a bowl. With wet hands, roll 2 teaspoons of mixture into a ball and place on a plate, covered with non-stick baking paper. Repeat with remaining mixture. Cover and chill for 30 minutes.

Make consommé: Heat oil in a large saucepan, and gently fry chilli strips for half a minute to seal juices. Add stock and bring to the boil. Gently place chicken balls into the saucepan. Reduce heat and simmer for about 5 minutes. The dumplings will be cooked when they rise to the surface.

Reserving a little for garnish, divide shredded spinach leaves into equal portions and place into soup bowls. Ladle soup and chicken dumplings into the bowls and garnish with remaining spinach and strips of red capsicum.

(SERVES 4)

French Onion Soup

SOUP
2 tablespoons olive oil
2 tablespoons butter
7–8 medium brown onions, thinly sliced
2 cloves garlic, crushed
½ level teaspoon sugar
5 cups vegetable stock
1 cup dry white wine
2 tablespoons Cognac (optional)

salt and freshly ground black pepper,
   to taste
1 cup grated Gruyère cheese

CROUTONS
1 baguette
olive oil spray or 1 tablespoon olive oil
1–2 cloves garlic, crushed

Make soup: Heat oil and butter in a large saucepan until butter melted. Add onions, garlic and sugar and gently stir until onions begin to colour. Continue cooking over very low heat for about 30 minutes until the onions have caramelised. Add stock, white wine and pepper and stir well, ensuring the base of the saucepan has been scraped. Bring to the boil, reduce heat and simmer, uncovered, for about 1 hour. The soup can be made ahead of time and refrigerated. When ready to serve, add Cognac, if desired. Bring back to the boil and simmer for a few minutes.

Make croutons: Preheat oven to 180°C. Line a baking tray with baking paper. Cut baguette into 2½cm diagonal slices to make 8 large or 16 small croutons. Spray or drizzle olive oil onto both sides of each slice of bread. Spread crushed garlic over one side and bake in oven for approximately 15 minutes or until crispy.

Just before serving, preheat grill on high. Fill bowls with hot soup. Gently float croutons on the surface and sprinkle thickly with Gruyère. Place bowls under hot grill until cheese is golden. Serve immediately.

(SERVES 6–8)

Gazpacho

SOUP

5–6 medium firm ripe tomatoes, roughly chopped or 2 x 400g tins diced peeled tomatoes, chilled

2 medium red capsicums, roughly chopped

1 medium red onion, roughly chopped

1 firm Telegraph cucumber, peeled and roughly chopped

3 sticks celery, trimmed and roughly chopped

4 cups (1 litre) tomato juice, chilled

1 clove garlic, crushed

1 cup white wine or ¼ cup red wine vinegar

¼ cup olive oil

1 teaspoon Tabasco sauce

salt and freshly ground black pepper, to taste

GARNISH

½ cucumber, finely diced

½ red capsicum, finely diced

¼ red onion, finely diced

sprigs of parsley, chives

croutons

Pulse all soup ingredients 2–3 times in a blender. (Process further for a smoother consistency.) Season with extra salt if required. Chill well. To serve, combine cucumber, capsicum and onion together. Divide gazpacho equally between 8 bowls and garnish. (SERVES 8)

Fruity Summer Variations

MANGO GAZPACHO

Substitute 2 heaped cups of fresh diced mangoes and 2 cups of orange juice for the tomatoes and tomato juice and 3 tablespoons fresh lime juice for the vinegar.

WATERMELON GAZPACHO

Substitute 2 heaped cups of fresh diced watermelon and 2 cups of orange juice for the tomatoes and tomato juice and 3 tablespoons fresh lime juice for the vinegar.

Papas Rellenas: Stuffed Potatoes

6 medium-sized potatoes
salt, to taste
1 egg
3 tablespoons plain flour

extra plain flour for rolling
250g block cheddar cheese
1 cup light olive oil

Make potato dough: Peel and dice potatoes into small cubes and place in a large saucepan, covered with water. Boil and when soft, drain potatoes in a colander. Allow potatoes to become dry to ensure mixture will not be watery. Return potatoes to the saucepan and mash them well until very smooth, adding salt to taste. Set aside to cool a little, but still warm. Add egg and flour and mix well.

Cut cheese in sticks, about 6cm x 1cm.

Make stuffed potatoes: Prepare a baking tray sprinkled with flour. Sprinkle extra flour on a small plate, in preparation for rolling. Coat your hands with flour. Place 3–4 tablespoons of the potato mixture in the palm of one hand and flatten it a little with the other. Place a stick of cheese in the centre and enclose it until completely covered with the potato, to form a 2cm x 10cm piece. Gently roll it on the prepared plate and place on the baking tray. Repeat using the remaining potato mixture and cheese, making sure your hands are always coated with enough flour to prevent sticking.

Heat oil in a 23cm non-stick frying pan. When oil is hot, fry potatoes on one side until golden and turn over to fry other side. Keep the oil hot for a crispy potato shell. Drain on a paper towel. Serve immediately while cheese is still hot inside. Serve with a green salad.

(SERVES 6; MAKES 12 PIECES)

Potato Curry Puffs

1kg potatoes, peeled and diced
1 tablespoon vegetable oil
3 small brown onions, diced
1½ cups frozen baby peas
2½ tablespoons curry powder
1 egg, lightly beaten

5 sheets frozen puff pastry, defrosted in
   the refrigerator
olive oil spray
sesame seeds or poppy seeds, to garnish
chutney or yoghurt, to serve

Make filling: Boil potatoes until just beginning to soften. Drain and cool. Heat oil and fry onions until golden. Gently combine potatoes, onions, peas, curry powder and egg in a large bowl.

Prepare puffs: Cut each pastry sheet into six equal pieces. Place a large spoonful of filling in the centre of each piece of pastry. Fold pastry over filling and press along seam to seal, forming rolls open at each end. Place seam side down on a greased or baking paper-lined oven tray. Refrigerate until ready to bake.

Preheat oven to 180°C. Spray rolls with oil and sprinkle with seeds. Bake for about 15 minutes, until golden. Serve with chutney or yoghurt.

(MAKES 30 PIECES)

~

Rice Paper Spring Rolls

150g thin rice or vermicelli noodles
1 teaspoon sesame oil
1 tablespoon lime or lemon juice
2 tablespoons sweet chilli sauce
24 rice paper sheets or rounds
2 red capsicums, finely julienned

2 carrots, finely julienned or coarsely
   grated
2 cucumbers, unpeeled, finely julienned
   coriander, 24 sprigs
Asian dipping sauce, such as soy or
   sweet chilli, to serve

Soak rice noodles in a large glass bowl of boiling water for 5–10 minutes, until tender. Drain and rinse under cold water. Gently stir sesame oil, lime juice and sweet chilli sauce through the noodles.

Half-fill a large bowl with warm water. Making 6 rolls at a time, dip a sheet of rice paper into the bowl until just softened, spread it on a clean flat surface and pat dry. Place a small quantity of noodles, julienned vegetables and a sprig of coriander into the centre. Gently fold the bottom of sheet up over the filling, then fold each side toward the centre, rolling as tightly as possible without tearing the wrapper. Place seam-side down on a plate. Repeat the process.

Serve with dipping sauce.

(MAKES 24 ROLLS)

Spinach Soup

A favourite recipe of US senator Joseph Lieberman and his wife Hadassah

1kg fresh spinach, washed, stalks
 discarded
1 cup water
salt and freshly ground pepper, to taste

½ cup parmesan cheese, grated
4 tablespoons plain yoghurt
½ lemon
4 thin lemon slices

Bring the water and a pinch of salt to the boil in a large saucepan. Add spinach and push down until wilted, yet still bright green. Drain and reserve water and allow spinach to cool. Process half the spinach and half the parmesan cheese together in a blender until smooth. Repeat with remaining spinach and parmesan cheese. Thin the blended mixture with reserved water to achieve desired consistency. Taste and add salt and pepper, as required.

Serve hot or cold with a squeeze of lemon juice, garnished with a dollop of yoghurt and a slice of lemon.

(SERVES 4)

~

Watermelon & Feta Bites

¼ seedless watermelon
1 x 200g block smooth feta cheese
24 chives
200g rocket leaves

salt and freshly ground black pepper
1 lemon, juiced (optional)
2 tablespoons lemon-infused olive oil
1 tablespoon balsamic vinegar

Cut watermelon into 24 pieces, about 5cm x 3cm.

To ensure feta doesn't crumble, plunge a sharp knife into a container of boiling water. Slice block of cheese in half and then into 5cm x 3cm pieces. Place a piece of feta on top of each piece of watermelon, tie up with a chive and refrigerate until ready to serve.

In a separate bowl, toss rocket leaves with salt, pepper, lemon juice and most of the olive oil. Place 4 watermelon and feta bites on each plate and accompany with serving of salad. Drizzle with remaining olive oil and balsamic vinegar.

(SERVES 6)

Something Savoury

- Granny Bee's Pickled Vegetables
- Strawberry & Baby Spinach Salad
- Tofu Fingers with Sweet Chilli Sauce
- Rakott Krumpli: Hungarian Scalloped Potatoes
- Gnocchi with Fines Herbes & Tomato Sauce
- Bowties with Kasha & Mushrooms
- Tomato Rice
- Russian Breakfast Omelette
- Very Wild Rice & Corn Salad
- Sundays' Best – Bagels & Toppers
- Tuscan Lentils
- Humble Gem Squash
- Asian Omelette Salad; Spinach & Currant Salad
- Avocado & Chickpea Salad; Green Mango Curry
- Crustless Spinach Tart
- Mango & Spinach Salad; Rhona's Spaghetti & Cheese
- Onion Flan with Potato Crust; Spicy Orange Salad
- Middle Eastern Rice with Noodles; Mediterranean Omelette
- Roasted Red & Yellow Tart; Watermelon Salad
- Snow Pea & Pear Salad; Viennese Cucumber Salad
- Truffled Polenta
- Caramelised Onions & Tomatoes
- Tomatoes Provençale; Roasted Truss Tomatoes
- Bagel Toppings: Anchovy Spread; Liptauer Spread
- Crunchy Cabbage Salad with Lemon Dressing

JOANNE FEDLER

Joanne Fedler is the author of many books including *The Dreamcloth, Secret Mothers' Business* and *When Hungry, Eat.*

She grew up in Johannesburg, South Africa, graduated with an LLM from Yale in 1993 as a Fulbright scholar, and taught law in South Africa before setting up a legal advocacy centre to end violence against women.

As co-director of Moonstone Media, in 2006 Joanne helped publish *A Pocketful of Sequins*, a book of inspirational quotes by women with breast cancer, all proceeds of which go towards breast cancer research. Her book, *When Hungry, Eat,* explores the themes of emigration, spirituality and our relationship with food.

Joanne lives with her husband and children in Sydney, Australia, where she writes, cooks, and takes early-morning runs along the beach.

The Pickle Queen

The first time I ever tasted a pickle I must have been about four. I was sitting at my granny's dining-room table.

My granny, Berenice Verita Cumes (née Fenhalls), wore bed-jackets, crocheted water-bottle covers and made hand-knitted booties with embroidered rosebuds for newborn babies. She always urged me to sip her whisky, and never forgot to give me pocket money.

She let my sisters and me put on her hot-pink lipstick that smelled of powder and sweetness. She let us play 'house' with her silverware, some of which had little pewter angels on their handles. She even had egg-cups that were shaped like water lilies. She insisted on good manners, particularly 'not licking your knife and keeping elbows off the table', and she brushed our hair until it looked like a 'silken curtain'. She let us powder ourselves with her large powder-puff and fed us liquorice, wine-gums and marshmallows as rewards for beautiful manners.

She was a shocking driver, nervous and twitchy, constantly applying the brake immediately after the accelerator. Driving with her always made me nauseous. She told us stories of when she was a young woman and as beautiful as a film star. She reminded us – over and over again, each time as if it were the first – that Syd James from the *Carry On* movies (who was South African, you know) was one of her (many) boyfriends. Of boyfriends, she had never been short. She could still charm a boy of eighteen, even when she was in her seventies and eighties. 'Isn't he gooooorgeous?' she'd say.

My granny was elegant and petite and didn't look like a marvellous chef; I always imagined them to be large and ruddy. She wore high-heels even in the kitchen. But she was a wonderful cook. She made her own pickles in huge jars: chunky wedges of onions and cucumbers, cauliflower, carrots and peppers, the gaps filled with a vinegar made with peppercorns, bay leaves, coriander seeds and garlic.

I liked the cauliflower best for its squeaky crunchiness. I also loved to eat the cucumbers; I would suck out the soft inner ring of seeds and stick the cucumber on my finger like a ring. Then I'd nibble off the dark green skin and finally get to the crispy white flesh. My whole mouth would pucker, my cheeks clench, and my taste-buds sit upright as the combination of the sour vinegar, sweet sugar and salty brine had their way with my mouth. My granny called me 'the Pickle Queen' and warned that if I ate too many, I'd grow a pickle tree in my tummy.

16

Pickled Vegetables.

Mix together
1 Cauliflower c in flowerettes
2 fresh cucumbers sliced
1-2 carrots sliced
1-2 green peppers thick slice
1-2 onions chunked

Then boil together
1½ cups white vinegar
2½ cups water, 3 tbs sugar.
2 tsp. salt . 6 or 8 Bay
leaves . 10 peppercorns
a few bits of garlic (n'salt)
few coriander seeds.
Pour hot over vegetables
which have been put in
to glass jars. Leave to
pickle for 2 days & then eat

top: Handwritten recipe by
Joanne Fedler's Granny Bee.

right: Granny Bee.

ONE EGG IS A FORTUNE

But once I started, I couldn't stop. Some people are born with a sweet tooth. I was born with a pickle tooth. I'll go for a pickle over a chocolate any day. Left alone with a jar of pickled onions, I have been known to eat them down to the very last one and then drink the vinegar, the only tell-tale signs my onion breath and my white pickled lips.

For me, the party only starts when the pickle pitches up – whether it's a dull hot-dog, the average hamburger, brisket on rye, pastrami on sourdough, smoked salmon on bagel, cheese on bread … add the pickle and you have yourself a whole new effect. A pickle brings out the dance of flavours in just about any washed-out party-pooping ingredient.

Whenever I eat a pickle, I think of my Granny Bee who was, in truth, herself the Pickle Queen.

My granny was elegant and petite and didn't look like a marvellous chef; I always imagined them to be large and ruddy. She wore high-heels even in the kitchen. But she was a wonderful cook.

Granny Bee's Pickled Vegetables

From Granny Bee's treasured hand-written recipe book

1 small head cauliflower, cut into florets

2 large cucumbers, sliced

2 carrots, sliced

1 green capsicum, cut into chunks

1 red capsicum, cut into chunks

2 onions, cut into chunks, or 8 tiny
  pickling onions

PICKLING INGREDIENTS

4½ cups white vinegar

4½ cups water

10 tablespoons white sugar

6 teaspoons salt

8 bay leaves

20–30 peppercorns

4–5 cloves garlic, finely sliced

1 tablespoon coriander seeds

Place vegetables into a large jar. These can be mixed or layered in colours. Boil all vinegar ingredients and pour over the vegetables. Allow to cool, seal and place in the refrigerator to pickle for 2 days.

GAVIN FINGLESON

Gavin Fingleson is a professional sportsman.

He was born in 1976 in Johannesburg, South Africa, the son of Frank and Cheryl.

Gavin began playing baseball at the age of five, emulating his grandfather, father and older brother Larry. He also played state soccer and state tennis.

After emigrating from South Africa to Sydney, Australia, in 1987 with his parents, Gavin started playing baseball for the Australian team at the age of fifteen, winning a silver medal at the Athens Olympic Games in 2004. He has been named State Maccabi Sportsman of the Year three times and has twice received the Maccabi Australia Sportsman of the Year award as Australia's most outstanding Jewish athlete. Gavin continues to be involved in baseball, sport and fitness.

Gavin is married to Julie Feller and they have two children.

The 'Turkey Sandwich' Boy

I have never played with Jewish baseballers. Everyone playing college baseball in Alabama and Louisiana was generally Catholic. Food would be provided by the home team. The staple diet was sandwiches and pizza – ham and pineapple or supreme – all non-kosher.

My first game on the road was not good. I chose not to eat the non-kosher food and had to survive on protein drinks. I made a mental note to organise alternative food but I forgot and in came the pizzas – same as usual. I went to the clubhouse manager – the guy who cleans and washes the uniforms – and asked him for sandwiches. 'But there is pizza,' he said. 'I can't have it, I'm Jewish,' I told him. Now this was down south and it was hard to explain our dietary rules such as not eating pork. I was starving and promised to explain it all later. He prepared what was left over: lettuce, tomato and mayonnaise on two white rolls – a straight artery blocker.

The next day before we left, I spoke with the manager and asked him to call ahead to organise the food. 'If we stop anywhere, this is what I can and can't eat,' I told him. 'Turkey and salad is fine, but no cheese.' Finished the game, got to another place, and lunchboxes were passed around on the bus. My coach said that my name should be on a bag. I walked up and down the aisle asking the guys what they were eating – ham and cheese. I spotted a bag with 'Gavin' on it; it was already half-eaten. 'Give my food back,' I said. Sure enough, the ribbing started: 'kosher boy', 'kosher food'; this went on throughout the season. Everyone labelled me the 'turkey sandwich'.

Although one of the respected captains and a team player, I was also the team clown. Everyone knew they could joke with me. But when one or two guys said something derogatory about my religion, I had to pull them up.

In professional baseball it was a little better but there were the same food issues. After the first match, I again had to approach the club manager. Pasta with ricotta cheese, regular cheese and tomato sauce was organised. At the end of each game I would stay outside and sign autographs for 45 minutes; the kids were there to watch us and I would be there for whoever came. The other players would come straight in, have a few beers and devour the spread. 'My food' was occasionally eaten; it got a little hairy once or twice in the locker-room. If we were winning, a better spread was provided and I would get my pasta with spinach mixed in. These were the times I missed home and my mom's cooking!

left: Gavin and Julie at their wedding (Sydney, Australia, December 2004).

below: Gavin as a schoolboy (aged five, Johannesburg, South Africa).

above: Gavin playing baseball (Athens, Olympics Games 2004, silver medallist).

Exciting moments at the Olympics 2004

Walking into the stadium at the opening ceremony, my parents and brother in the audience, was unbelievably exciting. Until you've experienced it, you can't grasp what it's like: a sea of athletes, the roar of the crowd and looking up at 80,000 people. 'Wow!' I said to my teammate, 'look for C24 upper level; my parents are there. My dad has been to every game since I was four years old.' When the Australian team curled into the middle of the stadium, I saw my dad in a black shirt. I started dancing. My mum, who never gets up to dance, stood up with my dad and brother and started dancing. I realised how close our family is and how supportive they have been. I was emotional and a tear appeared in my eye!

Winning against Japan in the semis, giving us a chance of a gold medal against Cuba, was another exciting and emotional moment. Baseball is a team game: you win together, you lose together and I contributed to our team. I made that last play. It felt like ten thousand pounds had been lifted off my shoulders. I stood there for a few seconds until the guys started jumping on me. We had a silver medal!

Standing on the podium is the flip-side, the emotional side. Why do you cry? In the beginning, you hold your tears back and your head high. I reflected on the many years I have committed to this sport and here I am getting a wreath and a silver medal. My mother told me to 'stop and smell the roses'. Once again, I looked at my parents and then I lost it and cried there on the podium.

I saw my dad in a black shirt. I started dancing. My mum, who never gets up to dance, stood up with my dad and brother and started dancing. I realised how close our family is and how supportive they have been. I was emotional and a tear appeared in my eye!

Strawberry & Baby Spinach Salad

A colourful dish prepared by my mother Cheryl

1 avocado
1 lemon, juiced
150g baby spinach
250g punnet small strawberries, halved
½ red onion, thinly sliced
100g crushed sugared **Vienna** almonds
    or sesame bars (optional)

RED WINE VINEGAR DRESSING
½ cup castor sugar
1 teaspoon Worcester Sauce
¾ cup olive oil
½ cup red wine vinegar
1 teaspoon poppy seeds
1 teaspoon sesame seeds
½ teaspoon dry mustard powder
½ teaspoon sweet paprika

Make dressing: Place all dressing ingredients in a screw-top glass jar and shake well or place in a blender.

    Make salad: Peel avocado, slice into fans and drizzle with lemon juice to prevent discolouration. Layer baby spinach, strawberries, avocado and onion on a platter. Pour over the dressing and sprinkle with crushed almonds.

(SERVES 4–6)

GARY FRIEDMAN

Gary Friedman is an internationally renowned producer, director and puppet performer.

He has over thirty years' experience working on educational puppetry and live theatre programs in Africa, Canada, Australia and Europe.

Gary was born in 1956 in Cape Town, South Africa. Puppetry fascinated him from an early age. After studying drama at the University of Cape Town, he obtained a French government scholarship to further his puppetry skills in France.

From 1987 to 1997, Gary's projects tackled controversial and sensitive issues such as HIV/AIDS, abuse and domestic violence. His best-known shows include *Puppets Against Abuse, Puppets in Prison* and *Puppets Against AIDS*, the latter running for more than ten years.

Gary produced and directed the television series *Puppet Election '94*, a political satire of the first South African democratic elections. In the late '90s, he co-produced a daily educational children's television series, *The Pezoolies*, in six local languages. More recently, he has produced and performed *The Losh 'n' Horror Show* and *Looking for a Monster* in South Africa, Kenya and Australia.

Gary migrated to Sydney, Australia, in 2002 with a Distinguished Talent visa from the Australian government and obtained his citizenship in March 2005.

Currently Gary runs a visual theatre and puppetry-in-education consultancy at the Seymour Theatre, University of Sydney. He is married to Sharon and they have one son.

French Flair

I studied puppetry at the Institute Internationale de la Marionnette in Charleville – Mézierès, a major international puppetry centre in the Ardennes region of France. The Meuse River meanders nearby and the valley is closed off by thick forests.

While many people come to the puppet performances held every summer, the special event is the Festival Mondial des Théâtres de Marionnettes, one of the largest puppet festivals in the world and held every three years. As many as 150 professional troupes perform more than fifty shows a day on the streets and in every available space in the town. Tickets are cheap and shows are for adults as well as children.

While in France, I became aware of the difference between living and existing, and accepted the philosophy that life, like the theatre, should be adventurous without risk – *la théâtre doit risqué, sans le risqué.*

What risk? Too many of my friends, my age and younger, have been diagnosed with cancer. We are eating mercury in fish, antibiotics in meat, chemicals and processed foods. After America, Australia has the highest rate of obesity in the world. People let their children consume fatty foods and sweet fizzy drinks but do not allow them to tattoo or pierce their bodies. What is worse?

I am a vegetarian; I haven't eaten meat or fish for thirty years. I follow a macrobiotic diet and believe that food and food quality affects our health, our wellbeing and our happiness. Of course, it was not easy being a vegetarian in France but it was always possible to order *crudités*, a traditional French appetiser of raw vegetables sometimes soaked in vinaigrette and a bottle of red wine.

In Charleville – Mézierès, a market operates twice weekly at the 17th-century Place Ducale in the centre of town. The atmosphere is wonderful. Stalls with their canvas canopies are set up to display the local produce. The regional specialities are smallgoods, wine and cheeses, including my favourites, the creamy Chaource, Langres and Rocroi. The merchants, dressed in white overalls, animatedly sell their wares, calling out and even singing. I was enchanted by the small cafés, food shops and pâtisseries – there is nothing quite like the aroma of fresh bread! Enticed, I would buy a baguette, cheese and fruit and have a picnic in the park.

Tofu Fingers with Sweet Chilli Sauce

An appetising alternative

TOFU FINGERS

300g firm tofu

¼ cup soy sauce

1 small knob ginger, grated

2 cloves garlic, crushed

1 sprig thyme (optional)

½ lemon, juiced

1 cup plain flour

2 eggs, lightly beaten

1 cup breadcrumbs (sesame seeds or cornflake crumbs can be substituted)

olive oil, for frying (optional)

DIPPING SAUCES

sour cream

sweet chilli sauce

Tofu fingers can be baked or fried. If baking, preheat oven to 180°C.

Make tofu fingers: Cut tofu into 24 finger-sized pieces. Combine soy sauce, ginger, garlic, thyme and lemon. Marinate tofu in this mixture for 30 minutes, turning occasionally.

Place tofu on a paper towel and cover with a second paper towel to absorb excess moisture. Dip tofu first in flour, then in beaten egg, and finally in breadcrumbs. Chill for 30 minutes to set coating.

Pan-fry tofu fingers in a little olive oil or bake on a lined tray until golden brown.

Serve with dipping sauces.

(MAKES 24 PIECES)

ALAN GOLD

Alan Gold is an Australian novelist, literary critic and human rights activist.

He was born in 1945 in Leicester, United Kingdom, the son of Alex and Ada.

Despite studying science, Alan always wanted to be a journalist. He became a reporter, specialising in politics and travelling throughout the United Kingdom and Europe. He settled in Israel in the late 1960s, writing articles on Middle Eastern politics for international news agencies.

Alan and his Australian wife Eva moved to Sydney, Australia, in 1970. Alan combined a career in writing while setting up a business in marketing and consultancy. His first book, *The Pregnant Father*, was a bestseller. In 1992, *How to Market a Small Business* was a huge success and has subsequently been reprinted many times. His other books, many of which have been translated, include *The Jericho Files, The Lost Testament, The Final Candidate* and *Pirate Queen*. The trilogy, *The Gift of Evil, The Marmara Contract* and *Berlin Song*, developed from Alan and Eva's trip to Slovakia (Eva's birthplace) in 1996. *Minyan*, published in 1999, is an anthology of short stories.

Alan divides his time between writing and motivational speaking within the marketing and business world. He is a guest lecturer in literature, racism and human rights at Australian universities and a regular contributor to the *Australian* newspaper as well as Australian and international magazines. In June 2000, he was the NSW Human Rights Orator and the B'nai B'rith Human Rights Orator in Sydney and Melbourne. He is a past president of the Anti-Defamation Unit of B'nai B'rith.

Alan lives with Eva in the Blue Mountains just outside Sydney, Australia. They have three children.

Pure Gold

*T*el Aviv, Israel, 1970. I was working as a journalist for Reuters, the international newsagency. I had been living alone on Rechov Dizengof, the main street running through the city, and needed to ease the financial burden of residing in such a prime location. That was when David joined me. David had been my 'brother' on my kibbutz, Ma'ayan Zvi.

I was sitting in a café on Dizengof, counting my shekels, trying to calculate how I was going to pay my rent when David walked in. 'I've got nowhere to stay,' he announced. I stopped counting my shekels. 'If you share the rent, you can live with me forever!' Problem solved. He moved in and took over half the apartment.

Life, from then on, became a series of the most frustrating happenings imaginable. Why? Because David was good-looking, a tough, deeply tanned *sabra* (person born in Israel), a paratrooper, a frontline sergeant, and most importantly, he knew how to chat up women from England, Ireland, Scotland, Wales, America, from anywhere – as well as every female *sabra*. I, on the other hand, was a short, stocky asthmatic, a particularly unhealthy Englishman, who had only just survived six months of *ulpan* (a school for the intensive study of spoken Hebrew) on the kibbutz.

Unlike David, I often spent my evenings alone. But one particular evening is unforgettable. I could no longer listen to the noises in the adjoining bedroom as I was becoming totally unimaginably jealous, and see-sawed between feeling more and more disheartened and more and more angry. I escaped to visit a friend, a lady from Australia.

As we were talking, there was a knock on her front door. In walked Eva, a lovely young Australian woman. We were introduced, we shook hands. I watched her as she hung up her coat. I was mesmerised by her delicacy: the way she stood, the way her body moved. She was so sophisticated. I knew at that very moment that there was some powerful chemistry between us.

Thus began a new chapter in our lives. We would meet at Eva's bus-stop near her apartment every day and would travel to her work together. True romance! Our rapport was now solid and I finally plucked up enough courage to invite Eva to my apartment for dinner. You have no idea how broke I was and despite now sharing the rent, I was still counting my shekels. I literally had a handful of Israeli coins in the bank … penury and starvation. What to do?

I was so desperate to impress her, I emptied my bank account and went straight to the butcher to buy steak. Now, in Israel in 1970, steak was gold, serious stuff!

above: Haifa in 1972.
left: Tel Aviv in the early 1970s.

above: Eva and Alan Gold.

Eva had a beautiful complexion and I knew that fresh vegetables were needed for good health and her glorious Czech skin. So to further dazzle her, I purchased a variety of fresh vegetables.

The meal was superb – steak in red wine and onion sauce accompanied by my home-made ratatouille. We sat sipping wine in the candlelight. I suggested that maybe this was the sort of thing we should be doing for the rest of our lives. Eva agreed. We kissed and cuddled; this was love.

At the end of the evening as I walked Eva to the bus-stop, I realised I had told a huge lie. I had led her to believe that I was wealthy, a really good catch. I had to gently break it to her that I was totally impoverished. 'Darling, tomorrow I have to go to Haifa on business and I won't be able to see you.' Eva replied, 'That's fine. We will see each other when you return.' I continued, 'Well, could I borrow the bus fare to Haifa?' She realised that I had spent my last shekel on dinner.

In spite of everything, she loved me and married me. We have been together now for over 40 years. I remain the impoverished one in every respect to Eva – to her brilliance, to her decency, her morality and especially to her compassion. All I can offer her is charm and cooking the ratatouille.

We would meet at Eva's bus-stop near her apartment every day and would travel to her work together. True romance!

Rakott Krumpli: Hungarian Scalloped Potatoes

Heartstopper!

6 large potatoes (waxy variety such as *désirée*)

2 teaspoons butter

1 or 2 large onions, thinly sliced

1 teaspoon paprika

4 eggs, hardboiled and grated

2 tablespoons finely chopped flat-leaf parsley

½ cup tasty cheese, grated

salt and freshly ground black pepper

6 tablespoons sour cream

extra butter

Preheat oven to 200°C.

Grease a 6-cup gratin dish with butter. Peel potatoes, slice very thinly and pat dry.

Melt 2 teaspoons butter in a small pan and fry onions until golden. Add paprika, mix well and set aside to cool. Stir through grated eggs, parsley and cheese and season with salt and pepper. Evenly arrange a third of the potatoes in the gratin dish. Spread half sour cream and half onion/egg mixture over potatoes. Repeat this finishing with a final layer of potatoes. Dot the top with butter. Cover with aluminium foil and bake for 45 minutes. Remove cover and bake for a further 15 minutes until top is golden. Allow to rest for a few minutes before slicing.

Note: For a contemporary dish, bake in 6 individual ramekins (½ cup size), greased with butter.

(SERVES 6)

Australia: a land abounding in
nature's gifts...

DAVID HELFGOTT

David Helfgott is a world-acclaimed Australian pianist.

He was born in 1947 in Melbourne, Australia, one of five children. His parents Rachel and Peter had emigrated from Poland after World War II.

David began playing the piano at a young age; he was a child prodigy, his musical gift being recognised at the age of five. His family moved to Perth and he continued to study piano, winning many competitions and awards. David moved to London to study at the Royal College of Music in his teenage years. During this time, he began showing signs of anxiety. He returned to Perth in 1970 and married his first wife, Clara, in 1971. After his marriage failed, David underwent many years of treatment and no longer performed. He met astrologer Gillian Murray in 1983 and a few months later they married.

After an absence from performing, David made a triumphant return to the world of classical piano in Australia and Europe. His life-story inspired the 1996 Oscar-winning movie *Shine*, starring Geoffrey Rush.

David and Gillian live in 'The Promised Land', a beautiful valley near Bellingen in NSW, Australia. He continues to perform concerts at his home and for charity.

An Italian Recital

The most exciting culinary experience I have had in the past few years was in the idyllic setting of Colleoli in the hills of Tuscany.

Shannon Bennett, the brilliant owner-chef of Vue de Monde in Melbourne, was staying with us at *Paretaio*, the villa owned by the well-known Australian artistic family, the Boyds. We had visited the house in 2004 and returned in 2005 for a relaxing pause in my busy performing schedule. We had a variety of friends visiting in June, and Shannon prepared many sumptuous meals for us.

One particular luncheon started with a fennel salad with blood orange dressing, followed by two different pastas: special bowties with olive oil, peas and anchovies; and gnocchi with a tomato fondue and buffalo mozzarella.

We then had the best wet polenta I have eaten, with porcini mushrooms, Grana Padano, truffle oil and sherry. It was utterly delicious. In fact, I had two helpings and even ate it whilst it was hot – I usually dawdle over my meals and don't always do the food justice, but this day I did.

The main courses were fish grilled on a very makeshift barbeque in a garden bed topped with a sage seasoning, and a roast with wild plums from the garden made into a piquant sauce.

To sit at the table made by Arthur Boyd in the very romantic logia attached to the house partaking of such marvellous food with people I love, was a sublime experience.

Gnocchi with Fines Herbes & Tomato Sauce

Fine fare

4 firm ripe tomatoes

120ml extra virgin olive oil

2–3 cloves garlic, peeled

salt and freshly ground black pepper, to taste

2 tablespoons finely chopped flat-leaf parsley

2 tablespoons finely chopped chives

2 tablespoons finely chopped French tarragon (optional)

shaved Grana Padano, for garnish

GNOCCHI

1kg potatoes, boiled in their skin then peeled

200g pasta flour*

150g Grana Padano, grated

10 sage leaves, finely chopped

2 large eggs

1 tablespoon olive oil

salt and freshly ground black pepper, to taste

Bring a large pot of water to the boil. Prepare a large bowl of iced water. Remove the stem from each tomato and cut an X at the bottom of each. Plunge the tomatoes into the boiling water for 10–20 seconds, until skins begin to wrinkle and loosen. Using a slotted spoon, gently remove the tomatoes and place into the ice bath to prevent further cooking. Beginning at the X, gently pull away the skins.

Slice the tomatoes width-ways into 6–10 rounds. Remove the seeds and julienne the flesh into 2–3cm strips. Place tomatoes, oil, garlic, salt and pepper into a saucepan. Bring to the boil, reduce heat and simmer for 5 minutes. Remove from heat and set aside.

Make the gnocchi: Mix all ingredients until just lightly combined. On a flat, dry work surface, flatten out to 2.5cm thickness and cut into squares. Bring a large pot of salted water to the boil and add a dash of olive oil. Drop gnocchi into water and cook for a few minutes until they float. Remove with a slotted spoon, drain well and place onto a serving platter.

Just before serving discard garlic from sauce and reheat gently. Remove from the stove, stir in fresh herbs and season to taste. Dress gnocchi with sauce and garnish with Grana Padano.

* Pasta flour, sometimes sold as type 'O' flour, is a high protein flour especially blended for making pasta by hand or in a domestic pasta machine.

(SERVES 4)

Recipe for Truffled Polenta – see page 146.

HERSCHAL HERSCHER

Herschal Herscher is a musician.

He was born in New York City, USA. His grandparents met there, each having immigrated from Europe. His father Manny was a schoolteacher and his mother Hilda worked as a travel agent.

Herschal inherited a love of music. His maternal grandfather Harry Cherkov played the fiddle with the Epstein Brothers. At the age of seven, Herschal started playing the piano accordion and this passion continued right through his high school years at Lafayette High in Brooklyn. At the age of eighteen, while studying at Brooklyn College, Herschal played piano professionally in a Latin–Cuban band with his brother David playing bass.

During his travels through Europe, Herschal met his future wife Linn Lorkin, an accomplished singer, in Paris. Herschal and Linn have a passion for *kletzmer*, Jewish folk music that originated in eastern Europe in the Middle Ages. Their band is called the Jews Brothers Band, a play on the renowned Blues Brothers.

Herschal and Linn have a son and live in Auckland, New Zealand.

The Borscht Belt

My family ran the Raleigh Hotel in the Catskills Mountains, a resort less than two hours from Manhattan. The Catskills, also known as the Borscht Belt, was where Jewish families vacationed and enjoyed musical entertainment and traditional cuisine. Most of the hotels in the Catskills were kosher and known as 'cultural resorts'. You had to register as a kosher hotel, and every now and then you would get inspected.

With two hundred rooms and what I thought was the best food and entertainment, the Raleigh was one of the most successful hotels in the area. It was just up from the huge Concord Hotel which boasted 1000-odd rooms! The staff at the Raleigh were incredibly loyal and many worked there most of their lives.

The big entertainment names of yesteryear, such as Danny Kaye, Sammy Davis Junior and Jerry Lewis, had their beginnings in the Catskills. The shows were typical Las Vegas-style interwoven with music slots.

During my summer vacations, I worked in various positions, as required, at the Raleigh. Jackie Mason would perform there every summer and on one occasion I was asked to help a bell-hop show Jackie to his backstage room. It was so exciting as he tried out a new routine on us. In my early teens I used to play both the piano and accordion with the visiting Latin bands, all very popular with the guests.

The kitchen jobs were something. We had to feed people three meals a day and you should have seen what they ate! After all, it was an all-inclusive holiday and as the food was free, you could order anything or everything on the menu. The menu changed every day except for *borscht* (beetroot soup), which was always available at lunchtime. This was the era when Americans adopted our food such as bagels and *blintzes* and *borscht*.

Sadly, the age of Jewish hotels in the Catskills is almost over. Where once there were hundreds of hotels, there are only a few left. And our family hotel, the Raleigh, has been sold.

Bowties with Kasha & Mushrooms

My mother was a great cook and I loved her kasha varnishke

2 tablespoons olive oil

1 large onion, diced

2–3 cups sliced button mushrooms

1 cup good quality whole **raw** kasha (buckwheat)

1 egg, lightly beaten

1 vegetable stock cube, dissolved in 2 cups boiling water

1 teaspoon salt

½ teaspoon freshly ground pepper

1 tablespoon margarine or butter

2 cups bowtie pasta, cooked and drained

flat-leaf parsley, finely chopped, to garnish

Heat oil, sauté onion until translucent and add mushrooms, allowing them to cook for 2 minutes.

Stir kasha and egg through and cook for 2 minutes, stirring constantly, until the kasha grains have separated.

Add hot vegetable stock, salt and pepper and bring to the boil. Reduce heat, cover and simmer for about 15 minutes until most of the liquid is absorbed. Remove from heat.

Allow to stand for a few minutes until the remaining liquid is absorbed. Add margarine and fluff with a fork.

Serve over a bed of bowtie pasta and garnish.

(SERVES 4–6)

RON KLINGER

108

Ron Klinger is a world-renowned bridge player, teacher and author.

He was born in 1941 in Shanghai, China, to Herta and Hermann. Both his parents had fled Vienna, Austria, in 1939 and later married in Shanghai. The family moved to Sydney, Australia, in 1946. Ron excelled in his studies at the University of Sydney and was awarded the University Medal for Law. He practised law for two years.

While lecturing and researching at the University of Sydney, Ron began teaching bridge at the NSW Bridge Association. Ron had always been an avid chess player but bridge became his obsession. In 1972 he left the university to take up bridge full-time.

Ron is an Australian Grand Master and World Bridge Federation International Master.

His contribution to bridge has been recognised by numerous awards including the BOLS Brilliancy Prize for Best Play at the World Bridge Championships in 1976, the BOLS Brilliancy Prize for Journalism at the World Bridge Championships in 1978 and 1980, honorary life membership Australian Bridge Teachers' Association 2003 for services to bridge, and IBPA Journalism Prize 2004.

Ron has written over fifty books ranging from bridge for children to highly advanced topics. One of Ron's personal literary highlights was winning the American Teachers' Association Book of the Year award for *Guide to Better Card Play*.

Ron continues to teach bridge and organise tournaments and bridge holidays. He is a regular columnist for the *Sydney Morning Herald*, the *Sun-Herald* and the *Australian Jewish News*.

He lives in Sydney, Australia, with his wife Suzie. The couple had two children, Ari and Keri, but sadly Keri passed away.

Bon Appetit!

*S*uzie and I were on our honeymoon in Italy. We went to a little restaurant for lunch in Pisa. We sat down and Suzie wanted to ask the waiter if anybody spoke English. I said, 'No, no! I know Italian!' We had been married only six months and this was our delayed honeymoon. I had studied Latin and thought that Italian could not be so different. Suzie pointed at the next table saying, 'Look, I'll have what that lady is having.' I explained to the waiter as best as I could and about fifteen minutes later, he returned with this black soup-like dish with something floating in the middle. 'What's that?' Suzie asked and the waiter answered in 'perfect' English, 'That's octopus in its own ink and that's what you ordered!'

~

Lunch-time bridge can be a dangerous game, since there are food and drinks as well as cards and scorers on the table. On one occasion, a lass was stuck for a lead during a lunch-time game. She inadvertently grabbed a sandwich and led that, giving declarer a ruff and discard at trick one.[1]

~

In 1980, the World Teams Olympiad was held in Holland in the resort town of Valkenburg. Players from fifty-eight countries were competing and the hotels were of the old-world variety. As there was no room service, the players came down to breakfast in the dining room each morning.

Over a series of breakfasts, the following was recorded:

A player from the East named Fazali came down to breakfast and sat opposite a French player.

'Bon appetit!' said the Frenchman.

'Fazali!' said the Eastern player, and that was the extent of the conversation.

The scenario was repeated next morning.

'Bon appetit!'

'Fazali!'

Later one of Mr Fazali's teammates took him aside and explained the meaning of 'bon appetit'. Next morning, Mr Fazali was ready when he came down to breakfast. He sat down opposite the Frenchman and proudly said: 'Bon appetit!'

'Fazali!' replied the Frenchman.

Adapted from Ron Klinger's The Bridge Player Who Laughed *(Modern Bridge Publications, 1994).*

---

1   A ruff and discard occurs when a player leads a suit that neither opponent has.

Tomato Rice

Another creation from my wife Suzie, a fabulous cook

2 tablespoons extra virgin olive oil
1 large onion, finely chopped
2 cloves of garlic, crushed
100g tomato paste

1½ cups basmati rice
salt to taste
4 cups water
50g pine nuts, lightly browned (optional)

Heat oil in a large non-stick saucepan and fry onions and garlic until soft but not brown. Stir in the tomato paste and allow to sizzle. Add water and salt and bring to the boil. Stir in the rice, return to the boil, reduce the heat and cover the saucepan. Cook on low for about 25 minutes, stirring every 10 minutes, until rice is tender. Garnish if desired.

Note: Vary the flavour by adding finely chopped red chilli and/or pitted olives at the same time as stirring in the rice. This dish can be served on its own or with chicken.
(SERVES 4)

Recipes for Caramelised Onions & Tomatoes, Tomatoes Provençale and Roasted Truss Tomatoes – see pages 146-147.

'When I heard the Star Spangled Banner, I thought about everything I went through to get here.'

LENNY KRAYZELBURG

Lenny Krayzelburg is a professional swimmer and an Olympic gold medalist.

He was born in 1975 in Odessa, Ukraine, the son of Oleg and Yelena.

He joined the Soviet Union's Olympic training machine and by the age of nine he was swimming up to five hours a day. In 1989, his family immigrated to the United States.

Lenny worked thirty hours a week at an aquatic centre to help support his family, in addition to his training. At age fourteen Lenny wanted to give up swimming but his father persuaded him to continue. By 1993, he was training at Santa Monica City College which helped him gain a scholarship to the University of Southern California where he majored in finance and investment. In 1996, he qualified for the Olympic trials.

Training solidly with an eye on the 2000 Sydney Olympics, Lenny won three gold medals and broke three world records at the Pan American Pacific Championships in August 1999 in the 50m, 100m and 200m backstroke. In the Sydney 2000 Olympics, Lenny won gold medals in the 100m backstroke, 200m backstroke and the 400m medley relay, breaking two Olympic records. Lenny held five world records in backstroke for long course and short course at one time.

Lenny was a commentator on Moscow television for the 2002 Short Course World Championships. He formed the Lenny Krayzelburg Foundation to support swimming for disadvantaged children in the inner city of Los Angeles. He has opened swim schools, and coaches and teaches at swim-stroke clinics.

Lenny met his wife Irina on a blind date in New York. They married in March 2005 and have twin daughters.

Fuelling an Olympic Dream

Before the Soviet Union dissolved in 1991, everyone was employed by the government. My father Oleg worked in the food industry supplying fruit and vegetables to various restaurants. After immigrating to America he worked in kitchens, first in a restaurant and then in a hospital.

Dad was a terrific chef, a real natural. For him, cooking was not a task but an enjoyable activity, even a passion. At home, Dad was the one in the kitchen. He is a very creative person, never using written recipes; the meal came from the head and heart. We always ate dinner together as a family. To this day, one of my favourite dishes is his chicken breast filled with mushrooms and vegetables, served with stuffed potatoes.

When I was training with Team USA, preparing for the Sydney 2000 Olympics, Dad would come over to my house and make breakfast for me before he went to work. The meal was wonderful – omelettes, oatmeal cereal, sausages and pancakes, all in very large quantities. Back then I wasn't conscious of my diet because weight wasn't an issue. But it has definitely become one now!

When I am training and travelling I long for Russian food, especially schnitzel and pastries. My dad and my wife Irina prepare the schnitzel in a special way – dipped in egg and then fried, almost like an omelette over meat. My mom Yelena makes recipes from our old home in Odessa – pastries with fruit and nut cakes that are seven layers high.

Eating Russian food is a social event, a five-hour meal. Once I invited some of my American teammates to a Russian restaurant. It was quite a culture shock for them. The food came in huge quantities – lots of meat, lots of fish, all highly seasoned with a variety of stuffing. Russian meals always consist of many courses. In America, if you order one appetiser, you are served one appetiser. In a Russian restaurant, when you order one appetiser, you are served ten different trays of appetisers. At this point, you are quite satisfied but along comes soup and more courses, hot and cold. All in all, somewhere between seven or eight different entrées, mains and desserts are served, one more delicious than the next. My teammates really enjoyed it!

Russian Breakfast Omelette

Fit for a champion

1 tablespoon oil
5 medium potatoes, peeled and cut into
   small cubes
1 onion, finely chopped
1 tomato, diced

6 eggs
3 tablespoons milk
salt and freshly ground black pepper, to
   taste
fresh chives, snipped for garnish

Heat oil in a non-stick frying pan. Add the potatoes, cover, and cook for 10–15 minutes, until tender. Add onions and tomatoes and cook for a further 5 minutes. Beat eggs with milk, salt and pepper, pour over vegetables and cook until set. Garnish and serve.
(SERVES 4)

Brian Sherman AM is a businessman, entrepreneur, philanthropist and animal rights advocate.

BRIAN SHERMAN

He was born in 1943 in Brakpan, South Africa, the son of Hymie and Minnie. His father's family had left Lithuania in 1910 to escape persecution. Brian was educated at Krugersdorp Boarding School, Brakpan High and Princeton College. He met his wife Gene Tannenbaum while they were both studying at the University of the Witwatersrand. With a young family and virtually no money, Brian immigrated to Sydney, Australia, in 1976.

Brian established an independent funds management group, the EquitiLink Group, in 1981 with Laurence Freedman. They built Equitilink from a company with no clients into the largest independent fund management company in Australia. They sold it at the end of 2000.

In 2004, together with his daughter Ondine, Brian founded Voiceless, an organisation aimed at increasing public awareness about animal rights and alleviating their suffering.

Brian is the president of the Board of Trustees of the Australian Museum and is a director and/or chairman of a number of listed investment companies in the USA, Canada and Australia. He was a board member of the Sydney Organising Committee for the Olympic Games and a director of Channel Ten for some sixteen years. Brian is also heavily involved in numerous Australian and Jewish charities.

Brian was appointed a member of the Order of Australia 2004 for his service to the community as a philanthropist and benefactor to the arts, education and sporting organisations, and to business and commerce. He was the winner of the Ernst & Young Entrepreneur of the Year award – Eastern Region Champion of Entrepreneurship 2006.

Brian and Gene live in Sydney. They have two children and six grandchildren.

Innocent Creatures

My passion for animal rights began over 26 years ago, inspired by my daughter Ondine who was just seven years old at the time.

My mother Minnie used to live with us in Sydney. Once, when she was in the kitchen preparing the evening meal, Ondine looked up at her and asked, 'Gran, what are you cooking?' My mum replied, 'Tongue darling, for dinner tonight.' Ondine, looking confused and concerned said, 'What do you mean *tongue*? You don't mean, like, my tongue, somebody's tongue? Where does it come from?' And very matter-of-factly my mother said, 'From a cow, darling.'

This conversation changed our household. Ondine concluded that 'meat is animals and animals are meat'. It was the last time she ate red or white meat. I followed her example soon after. I am now a vegetarian, close to becoming a vegan. My wife Gene and son Emile are also vegetarians.

Over the years Ondine became passionate about animal rights. I supported her, having always had a strong kinship with animals. In 2003 we attended the annual Animal Rights Conference in Los Angeles. There were five hundred activists and sixty organisations, all with very little money. After listening and witnessing disturbing images of widespread animal suffering, especially in factory farms, for one full week, fifteen hours a day, we returned home absolutely devastated. This was a turning point in my life.

Voiceless was born in 2004 from this experience. Voiceless is a non-profit organisation that promotes respect and compassion for animals and aims to protect them from suffering. Our aim is to lift the veil of secrecy surrounding their maltreatment, especially with respect to factory farming. It is essentially a social justice movement. Our patrons include Nobel Prize-winning author J.M. Coetzee whose works include *Lives of Animals* and *Disgrace* which highlight human cruelty to animals.

Most people honouring the Yiddish writer and Noble Laureate Isaac Bashevis Singer (1904–91) are unaware that he was a vegetarian. This became a central theme in his work. 'The longer I am a vegetarian,' he wrote, 'the more I feel how wrong it is to kill animals and eat them. I think that eating meat or fish is a denial of all ideals, even of all religions. How can we pray to G-d for mercy if we ourselves have no mercy? How can we speak of right and justice if we take an innocent creature and shed its blood?' (From Isaac Bashevis Singer's short story, 'The Slaughterer'.)

Very Wild Rice & Corn Salad

A splash of colour

6 cups cooked basmati and wild rice
  mixture*

½ small red onion, finely chopped

1 cup diced red capsicum

1 cup corn kernels, fresh or tinned
  (drained)

½ cup finely chopped dried figs

⅓ cup chopped roasted cashews
  (unsalted)

⅓ cup chopped pecans

¼ cup finely chopped spring onions

DRESSING

4 tablespoons red wine vinegar

2 tablespoons lemon juice

1 garlic clove, crushed

2 tablespoon Dijon mustard

½ cup olive oil

1½ tablespoons caster sugar

salt and freshly ground pepper, to taste

Make dressing: Place all dressing ingredients in a screw-top jar and shake well.

Combine rice, onion, capsicum and corn in a large bowl. Just before serving gently toss figs, cashews, pecans, spring onions and dressing through the salad.

* If rice mixture unavailable, rice proportions should be 4 cups cooked basmati rice and 2 cups cooked wild rice.

(SERVES 6–8)

Sunny South Africa...

...a cornucopia of diverse scenery and cultures.

TALI SHINE

Tali Shine is a cosmetics entrepreneur, author and beauty editor.

She was born in 1982 in New Zealand and her family moved to Australia when she was two years old. Tali studied in Sydney and New York.

Tali is the author and co-illustrator of *The Glam Girl's Guide to Sydney Shopping*, *The Official Sydney Shopping Guide* and *The Glam Girl's Guide to New York Shopping*. Following the success of these titles, Tali became the official fashion ambassador for NSW Tourism and wrote their *Official Shopping Guide*. Tali's latest book is *Life: Spa*, which includes reviews of global retreat destinations such as Chiva-Som in Thailand, Cuixmala in Mexico, Gwinganna in Australia and The Ashram in the US.

From 2004-08, Tali was the fashion and beauty editor for *9 to 5 Magazine* and also wrote a weekly trend column that drew on her extensive experience as a columnist, fashion and lifestyle editor, stylist and model. Tali created her own range of cosmetics, *Tali by Tali Shine*, which was launched into David Jones stores nationwide. The range became a favourite of local and international celebrities.

Known for keeping her finger on the pulse of 'what's hot', Tali is frequently called upon by the media worldwide to comment on trends in fashion, beauty and travel including Vogue, Cosmopolitan, The Sunday Telegraph, A Current Affair, Qantas Q Air, and Fox 8.

Tali donates much time to charitable causes.

How Rituals Are Made

Our family's Sunday morning ritual began after a holiday in New York City. There are certain smells, tastes and colours that always take you back to a special time and place in your life.

One of our holiday's 'must dos' was to experience and savour traditional Jewish New York food. Our destination was Katz's Delicatessen and our mission was to taste their famed *lox* (smoked salmon) and cream cheese bagels. Nothing surpasses the aroma of freshly baked bagels.

Katz's Delicatessen in the historical Lower East Side was established by a Russian immigrant family in 1888. The deli continues to create the flavours of yesteryear and smatterings of Yiddish are still spoken.

We made the trek across town. The evening began in excitement and hunger but ended in tears – I accidentally dropped my bagel into the cold and dirty New York side street. By this time the deli had closed. What made the situation even worse was that we were leaving New York the very next day; no chance of going back and sampling another bagel. So my parents shared the remains of theirs with me.

On our return to Australia my family decided to try and recreate the bagel for our Sunday morning brunches. My parents would go to the Sydney fish markets to select the best quality smoked salmon of the day. Mum would be dropped home to heat the oven and prepare brunch with the fresh *lox,* cream cheese and salads while Dad would pick up the bagels from the kosher bakery in Bellevue Hill. While the bagels were being warmed, an intoxicating aroma filled our home. So each week we had the pleasure of reminiscing about Katz's Deli. For me, the best thing about this meal was there was no risk of dropping my bagel onto the sidewalk!

Sundays' Best – Bagels & Toppers

Try my Nanna's recipe — homemade bagels are the best!

BAGEL DOUGH

2 cups warm water

2 x 8g sachets dry yeast

3 tablespoons white sugar

6 cups plain flour

2 teaspoons salt

1 teaspoon vegetable oil

1 egg yolk

2 tablespoons milk or water

sesame seeds, poppy seeds or rock salt

Make dough: Combine water, yeast and sugar in a bowl and allow to stand for about 5 minutes until frothy. Slowly add 5 cups of flour and salt and mix together. Gradually add enough remaining flour to make a stiff dough, working it with your hands. Turn out onto a lightly floured surface and knead until smooth, adding more flour if required. Grease a large bowl with 1 teaspoon of the oil. Place dough in the bowl and cover. Leave in a warm place and allow to rise for 1–2 hours.

Make bagels: Place dough onto a flat surface and punch down. Divide into 12 equal pieces (or 24 pieces to make mini bagels). Form each piece of dough into a ball and roll each ball into 50cm lengths, joining the ends together **very firmly**. Ensure the hole is at least 2 fingers wide. (If making mini bagels, leave dough in balls and place the back of a wooden spoon through the ball.) Place the bagels on a lightly greased surface, cover with a clean cloth, and allow to rest and prove for about 20–30 minutes.

Preheat the oven to 180°C. Line a baking tray with baking paper.

Cook bagels: Bring 10 cups of water to the boil in a large pot and reduce heat. To prevent them from touching, simmer bagels in batches, turning each after 30 seconds until puffy on both sides. Remove with a slotted spoon and place onto baking tray. Mix together egg yolk and milk and use to lightly brush bagels. Sprinkle with sesame seeds or poppy seeds or rock salt. Bake for 5 minutes, then turn over and cook for a further 25–30 minutes until golden and skewer comes out clean. Remove from oven and allow to cool on a wire rack.

(MAKES 12 BAGELS)

Delicious toppers include Anchovy Spread and Liptauer Spread – see page 148 for recipes.

Other suggested toppers: cream cheese, capers, egg mayonnaise, herring, smoked salmon, trout mousse, avocado, fried diced onions, thin red onion rings, rocket, watercress, red capsicum strips, sundried tomatoes.

MARLENA SPIELER

Marlena Spieler is an internationally renowned chef, author and food columnist.

She was born in Sacramento, California, to Izzy and Caroline Smith. Having lived and travelled regularly around the world, Marlena broadcasts and writes about the food she has sampled and recreated, as well as techniques on its preparation.

Conjuring flavours and dishes from the Mediterranean to Mexico, California to France and the Italian islands, Marlena has written over fifty cookbooks published worldwide. *The Classic Barbecue and Grill Cookbook* was a bestseller in the United Kingdom.

Marlena has received many awards for her work. *Feeding Friends* won the 2000 International Cookbook Award in Perigueux, France, for Best Entertaining Cookbook in English and *The Jewish Heritage Cookbook* received the 2003 Special Jury Award at the World Gourmand Book Awards in the Loire Valley. She has been shortlisted for three prestigious James Beard awards (two cookbooks and a newspaper column) and two Guild of Food Writers awards (British radio and television). Marlena has won two Association of Food Journalist awards.

As a regular food columnist for many magazines such as *Bon Appetit Saveur Cooking Magazine* and *The Roving Feast*, Marlena insists, 'I just want to tell a good story, offer something to think about … give some good recipes and, in general, make readers feel good and get something of value.'

Marlena lives with her husband Alan in Hampshire, England.

If Life's Got You Down, Go to Umbria

If you're depressed, go to Umbria. If you can't shake a sniffly cold, think your haircut is the worst you've ever had, or if you're just in need of a little pick-me-up, go to Umbria.

If your husband or wife is being a pain, or your boyfriend or girlfriend has left you, if you have just walked off your job, can't stand breathing the filthy, smoggy city air around you, and you absolutely hate your living-room couch, go to Umbria.

Recently at my most stressed-out and depressed state of mind, with a bad haircut and what seemed like an endless case of sniffles, I was invited to the Ercole Olivios, the Academy Awards of Italy olive oil, where Italy's finest olive oil producers gather for judging, held in the little Umbrian town of Spoleto.

I wasted no time in packing my bag. Within hours of landing in Rome, I was passing through hill towns, heading for the enchanting walled town of Spoleto, and feeling perky as a kitten. Several days of tutored olive oil tasting lay ahead, with countless opportunities for eating and drinking, Umbrian style.

Suddenly I wasn't tense any longer, my sneezing had stopped, and even my haircut suddenly felt *bellissima*.

Umbria is Italy as one hopes it to be, but without the aggravation. It's Italy lite – you've got the culture, language and cuisine in a relaxed, laid-back, countryside setting with air so sweet it's a pleasure to just breathe. Even the driving seems sedate, as far as Italy goes.

Umbrian food is rustic, rustic even beyond Tuscan: seasonal vegetables and game, fabulous truffles eaten with the same gusto as equally fabulous lentils.

One day I was invited to lunch at *Casale Bartolini,* the Bartolini family farm, which spreads over a large mountainous region in the Nera River natural park.

The family grows fodder for the animals, legumes and grains of great delicacy, hunts for truffles in the winter, and cultivates groves upon groves of olives. The family has farmed this land since 1850 and, as Emilio Bartolini says, 'To be Umbrian means to be part of an olive oil culture.'

We ate outside, surrounded by the lush green hills of the Umbrian countryside, interspersing bites of rustic food with sips of homemade wine.

And, mouth full of these good things, I tried to remember exactly what it meant to be stressed out and tense.

Umbria is Italy as one hopes it to be, but without the aggravation. It's Italy lite — you've got the culture, language and cuisine in a relaxed, laid-back, countryside setting with air so sweet it's a pleasure to just breathe. Even the driving seems sedate, as far as Italy goes.

above: Campo de' Fiori in Rome.

American in Paris Learns to Shop à la Française

'Taste these stuffed grape leaves. My mother rolls them herself using an old family recipe,' purred the dark, handsome olive-seller in the Paris marketplace as he held out a glistening green cylinder of leaf-wrapped rice.

Not only do I have a hard time resisting a pretty face, but a delicious-looking grape leaf? No way. And these were close to perfection, vine leaf-wise: tangy, shiny leaves tightly wrapped around an herby filling. I bought a containerful, along with oily-dry black olives, briny green ones and the spicy pickled cauliflower-pepper-carrot mixture from North Africa that I have pretty well become addicted to.

Then I trotted over to the other side of the marketplace to show Paule Caillat my treasures.

Caillat leads Promenades Gourmandes – a sort of cooking class and Paris food shopping trek cum induction into the mysteries of being Parisian. Students meet up with Caillat and a handful of other food lovers from all over the world at a café in Paris's stylish Third Arrondissement and discuss, over a café au lait or espresso, what they all might like to learn about in the class to follow. Then the fun begins as she herds them around like so many errant children.

When I caught up with her, Caillat was in the middle of interrogating the fishmonger and, if I'm not mistaken, interrogating the fish as well. Both appeared to be giving in to her persuasion. Finally she found a sea bream that was just perfect, and as the fishmonger was wrapping it up, I opened my vine leaves.

'Taste them,' I said. 'The Olive Man's mother makes them herself.' I was chewing happily, thinking of a little woman, dressed in black, stuffing and rolling her leaves, contentedly sitting in her son's kitchen.

'Well, Marlena,' the voice of reality replied, 'these are delicious, but I hate to tell you that his mother died years ago. He has many stories. Don't believe a word. But his food – his food is always delicious.'

Extracts from The Roving Feast (San Francisco Chronicle, *2004 and 2005).*

Tuscan Lentils
A taste of Umbria

300g small, dark lentils (such as French Puy lentils)

4 cloves garlic, crushed

1 stalk celery, diced

4 tablespoons extra virgin olive oil

125g cured meat such as brisket, pastrami and smoked chicken/turkey, diced

¾ cup tomato passata or prepared tomato-based sauce

1 pinch red chilli flakes or 1 teaspoon finely chopped medium-hot fresh chilli

salt to taste

flat-leaf parsley, finely chopped for garnish

4 baby golden nugget pumpkins (optional)

Pour 2½ cups of salted water into a pot and add lentils. Add half garlic and half celery and bring it to the boil. Reduce heat and simmer for 35–40 minutes, or until the lentils are just tender but still firm.

Heat the olive oil in a large frying pan, sauté remaining celery, garlic and cured meat until lightly browned. Add the tomato sauce and chilli flakes, cooking for 10 minutes to blend flavours. Add lentils and their cooking water, and simmer over a low heat for about 10 minutes, adding more water if needed. If it's too soupy, raise the heat and cook down until thickened. Season with salt to taste.

If serving in pumpkin shells, preheat the oven to 180°C. Line a baking tray with baking paper. Cut off a reasonable-sized lid and scoop all the seeds out and discard.
Place pumpkins and lids onto tray and bake until soft but firm, 45 minutes to 1 hour.
Place pumpkins onto a serving plate and spoon in hot lentils.

Garnish with parsley.

(SERVES 4)

JANET SUZMAN

Janet Suzman is an actress and director.

She was born in 1939 in Johannesburg, South Africa, to Saul and Betty. Her childhood was divided between a family farm in Natal, the False Bay coast of the Cape, and school in Johannesburg. Janet left South Africa after completing a degree at the University of the Witwatersrand and moved to London in 1959 to train at the London Academy of Music and Dramatic Arts (LAMDA).

Her long career includes playing many of the major heroines for the Royal Shakespeare Company and in the West End, a notable Cleopatra and Masha amongst them. She has twice won the Evening Standard Best Actress Award and also Academy Award and Golden Globe nominations for Sam Spiegel's *Nicholas and Alexandra*. Other films include *The Draughtsman's Contract* and *The Singing Detective*. She worked with Fellini on *E La Nave Va* and her Hedda Gabler was chosen as the BBC's 50th Anniversary Classic Drama repeat.

Janet is the niece of Helen Suzman who famously opposed apartheid from a solitary opposition seat in the parliament of the day. Janet and her two brothers and sister left South Africa due to apartheid. Despite this, she never lost touch with the country and in 1987 directed and filmed *Othello* with John Kani at the Market Theatre in Johannesburg for Channel Four TV as a political protest play. She has written and directed her own response to Chekhov's *Cherry Orchard*, setting it in post-democratic South Africa, called *The Free State*. Her production of *Hamlet* from the Baxter Theatre, Cape Town, was invited to open the Royal Shakespeare Company's Complete Works Festival in 2006. *Coriolanus*, in which she played Volumnia, closed the ambitious year-long festival in May 2007.

Janet was married to Trevor Nunn for seventeen years and they have one son. She lives in London.

An Unwelcome Guest at the Sunday Roast

Many years ago when I was a small girl living in South Africa, my father went to South America and brought back some rare melon seeds. He had tasted the 'best melon he'd ever eaten' and was determined to grow them in our garden, a world away. He thought that South African temperatures must surely be akin to those found on the American continent. So, the seeds of this fruit were duly planted, and every day when my father returned from the office, it was to the vegetable patch that he first went to inspect their progress. They grew and grew and he was a happy man, looking forward to the day when they were big and ripe enough to pick and slice and eat.

One day the whole family – parents, two brothers and a sister – sat down happily to a Sunday lunch of roast beef, each of us ravenous and content with the world. The usual vegetables, bowls of crisp roast potatoes, green beans, gem squash, and a mysterious fourth offering – a weird pale-greenish mound covered in a white sauce – made their procession from place to place. You can guess: father's sweet melon had been picked and boiled and served up that day by our Zulu cook Minnie, thinking that a new kind of squash had appeared in her patch! The white sauce was her inspirational flourish to disguise the vile watery taste of the thing.

The penny suddenly dropped and a terrible roar erupted from the paternal throat. His precious exotic fruit had been downgraded to a mere over-boiled vegetable; it was too much for him! We all leaped up to prevent my father from dispatching poor Minnie from this world before her time.

When things had calmed down, the funny side of this culinary drama erupted – and Minnie in her kitchen breathed a long sigh of relief.

Humble Gem Squash

Prepared with no drama

3 baby gem squash,* washed
butter
salt and freshly ground pepper, to taste

Pierce the gem squash with a fork. Place squash in a pot of boiling water and cook until the green skin is tender. Remove using a slotted spoon, cut in half and place on serving plate and smother with lashings of butter and salt and pepper.

Note: Gem squash can be prepared in different ways – by boiling whole or in half, steamed or microwaved. The skin and seeds of a young gem squash are delicious but if preparing a mature gem squash, cut it in half and remove the seeds after cooking.

* Gem squash are from the squash family and are usually the size of a large onion. Squash is one of the oldest vegetables and is known to have been grown for over 6000 years by North American Indians.

(SERVES 3-6)

below: Gary Friedman, Puns en Doedie (Puppets Against Apartheid) early '80s, Cape Town.
below right: Gillian and David Helfgott.
middle right: Herschal Herscher, aged ten, playing the accordion.
far left: Brian Sherman with his older brother, Ron.

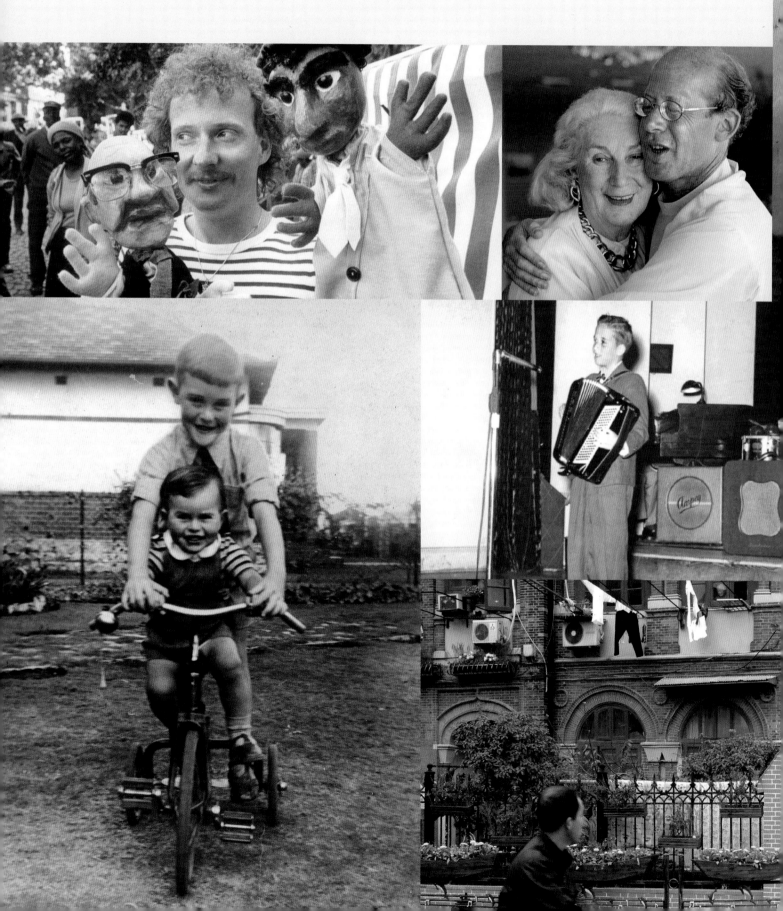

left: Tali Shine.

below left: Janet Suzman as a child.

above: Janet Suzman as Cleopatra.

left: Ron Klinger's childhood home, Shanghai.

Asian Omelette Salad

4 eggs, lightly beaten
1 tablespoon soy sauce
1 tablespoon finely chopped fresh parsley
1 tablespoon finely chopped fresh chives
2 carrots, peeled into long thin strips using a vegetable peeler
1 daikon (white radish), peeled into long thin strips using a vegetable peeler
6–7 red radishes, thinly sliced
1 cup bean sprouts
1 cup red cabbage, finely shredded
2 tablespoons pink pickled ginger, thinly sliced
4 spring onions, thinly sliced on the diagonal

ASIAN DRESSING
2 teaspoons wasabi paste (Japanese horseradish)
2 tablespoon mirin (sweet Japanese rice wine) or white vinegar
4 tablespoons soy sauce
2 tablespoons liquid from pink pickled ginger

Make dressing: Place all dressing ingredients in a screw-top jar and shake well.

Make omelette: Whisk eggs and soy sauce together and stir through parsley and chives. Heat a little oil in a 20cm non-stick fry pan over medium heat. Pour in half the egg mixture, tilting pan so that it coats base of pan. Cook for about 2 minutes until just set, slide onto a chopping board and roll up tightly. Prepare remaining mixture in the same way. Slice both rolls into 1cm rings.

Place carrots, daikon, radishes, bean sprouts, cabbage, ginger and ⅔ green onions in a large salad bowl. When ready to serve, gently combine dressing and vegetables. Garnish with omelette rings and remaining spring onions.

(SERVES 4)

~

Spinach & Currant Salad

2 tablespoons pine nuts
6 teaspoons currants
2 tablespoons lemon juice

150g baby spinach leaves
3 tablespoons olive oil

Toast pine nuts in a frying pan over medium heat until golden. Soak the currants in lemon juice for 5 minutes. Toss together with the baby spinach and pine nuts. Drizzle with the olive oil.

(SERVES 4)

Avocado & Chickpea Salad

1 x 420g tinned chickpeas, drained
   and rinsed
4 large Roma tomatoes, cubed
1 cup flat-leaf parsley, finely chopped
½ small red onion, finely chopped

2 tablespoons olive oil
salt and freshly ground black pepper,
   to taste
1 avocado
1 lemon, juiced

Dice avocado and place in lemon juice. Gently combine all ingredients in a large salad bowl and refrigerate.

   Note: Salad can be prepared in advance. Add avocado and lemon juice just before serving.

(SERVES 4)

~

Green Mango Curry

1 tablespoon oil
2 onions, chopped
1 cup roughly shredded coconut or ½
   fresh coconut, shredded
3 mild red chillies or ½ medium hot red
   chilli
2 cloves garlic, crushed
1 x 20cm knob ginger, grated

½ teaspoon ground cumin seeds
1 teaspoon dried coriander seeds or 2
   tablespoons fresh coriander, chopped
½ teaspoon ground turmeric powder
¾ teaspoon salt
3 large green mangoes, peeled and cubed
1 tablespoon brown sugar
1 cup water

Heat oil and fry onions until transparent. Blend coconut, chillies, garlic, ginger, cumin, coriander and turmeric. Add to the onions and stir-fry well, until oil begins to separate. Add mango, sugar, salt and water and cook until mangoes are tender and curry thickens. Serve with steamed rice.

   Optional: Shredded cooked chicken can be stirred through the curry.

(SERVES 4)

Crustless Spinach Tart

6 large eggs

½ cup milk

3 tablespoons plain flour or rice flour

½ cup mayonnaise

1 small red onion, finely chopped

500g frozen chopped spinach, thawed
and drained

1 cup shredded low-fat tasty cheese

salt and freshly ground black pepper,
to taste

½ cup shredded low-fat mozzarella
cheese

sweet paprika, to garnish

crisp green salad, to serve

Preheat oven to 180°C. Grease a 20 x 20cm baking dish.

Combine eggs, milk, flour and mayonnaise and beat until light and fluffy. Gently mix through onion, spinach, tasty cheese, salt and pepper. Pour into baking dish, sprinkle with mozzarella and paprika and bake for 35–40 minutes, until the centre has risen and set, and the top is golden.

Serve with a crisp green salad.

(SERVES 4)

Mango & Spinach Salad

50g pine nuts

1 x 425g tinned sliced mango

3 tablespoons heaped whole-egg
   mayonnaise

salt and freshly ground black pepper,
   to taste

120g baby spinach leaves

1 lemon

2 ripe avocados, diced and drizzled with
   lemon juice to prevent browning

Toast pine nuts in a frying pan over medium heat until golden and set aside. Drain mango juice into a small bowl and cut mango pieces into fine strips. Blend mango juice and mayonnaise until smooth, season with salt and pepper, set aside and refrigerate until ready to use.

Just before serving, layer half the baby spinach on a flat platter. Layer mango followed by avocado evenly over the top and repeat with remaining spinach, mango and avocado. Drizzle mayonnaise mixture over the salad and garnish with pine nuts.

(SERVES 6–8)

~

Rhona's Spaghetti & Cheese

100g unsalted butter

1 brown onion, chopped

2 cloves garlic, crushed

1 x 420g tin cream of tomato soup*

1 tablespoon Worcestershire sauce

375g spaghetti

1 cup grated cheddar cheese

Preheat oven to 180°C.

Melt 80g butter in a saucepan and sauté onion and garlic until soft. Add soup and Worcestershire sauce and stir well. Remove from heat and set aside.

Cook spaghetti in salted boiling water until just *al dente*, rinse and drain and place in a greased baking dish. Pour sauce over, sprinkle with cheese and dot with remaining butter. Bake for 30 minutes until the cheese has melted and top is golden and crisp. Serve with a green salad.

* 420g condensed tomato soup mixed with 185ml evaporated milk can be substituted for the cream of tomato soup.

(SERVES 4)

Onion Flan with Potato Crust

CRUST

2 cups grated raw potato

½ teaspoon salt

1 egg, lightly beaten

¼ cup grated brown onion

FILLING

olive oil spray

8 brown onions, diced

½ cup single cream

2 tablespoons butter

½ cup grated tasty cheese

1 egg, lightly beaten

salt and freshly ground black pepper,
to taste

Preheat oven to 220ºC. Grease a 23cm pie dish.

Make potato crust: Place grated potatoes and salt in a large bowl. Leave to stand for 10 minutes and then squeeze out excess water. Add remaining ingredients. Pat this mixture around base and sides of pie dish to form an even crust. Bake for 30 minutes, then spray top with olive oil. Bake for a further 10 minutes or so, until crust browns.

Make filling: Boil onions until soft and then drain well. Add cream, butter, cheese, egg, salt and pepper and mix well. Pour mixture into baked potato crust. Reduce oven temperature to 180ºC and bake for 20 minutes until set.

(SERVES 6)

~

Spicy Orange Salad

150g caster sugar

1 orange, juiced

1 lemon, juiced

½ teaspoon finely chopped medium-hot
fresh red chilli

½ teaspoon finely grated ginger

2 pink grapefruit

3 oranges

Place sugar in a small saucepan, cover with a little water and bring to the boil. Simmer until it just begins to change colour. Remove from heat and gently stir in the juices. When mixture has cooled completely, stir in the chilli and ginger.

Peel the grapefruit and oranges, ensuring all white pith has been removed. Slice, place in a glass bowl, pour over the spicy marinade and refrigerate for a few hours before serving.

(SERVES 4)

Middle Eastern Rice with Noodles

1 cup vermicelli egg noodles, broken into 1cm pieces

2 teaspoons olive oil

2 cups rice, uncooked

4 cups water or chicken soup, fresh or made using 1 stock cube dissolved in 4 cups boiling water

salt and freshly ground black pepper, to taste

1 large onion, diced

¼ cup pine nuts or slivered almonds freshly chopped flat-leaf parsley, to garnish

Heat 1 teaspoon olive oil in a large saucepan. Stir-fry noodles until golden, add rice and continue stirring until well mixed.

Add the water or soup, salt and pepper. Bring to the boil, turn down heat, cover and simmer for about 20 minutes, until rice is tender.

Heat 1 teaspoon olive oil in a non-stick frying pan and sauté onions until just golden. Add nuts and sauté until they begin to turn colour.

Fluff the rice and place into a serving dish. Garnish with onions, nuts and parsley.

(SERVES 4–6)

~

Mediterranean Omelette

150g marinated feta in oil

2 tablespoons oil from marinated feta

1 large red onion, cut into wedges

4 Roma tomatoes, cut into large chunks

25 pitted black olives

10 eggs

¼ cup chopped flat-leaf parsley

salt and freshly ground black pepper, to taste

150g baby cherry bocconcini

Preheat the grill.

Heat feta oil in a large non-stick frying pan. Fry onions until they begin to brown. Add tomatoes and olives and cook until just softened.

Whisk eggs, parsley, salt and pepper together in a bowl and pour into the frying pan.

Gently stir the mixture over a medium heat, until half-cooked and beginning to set. Sprinkle cheeses on top and place under the grill until the omelette is puffy and golden.

(SERVES 4–6)

Roasted Red & Yellow Tart

2 small yellow capsicums, quartered,
seeds and membranes removed
2 small red capsicums, quartered, seeds
and membranes removed
6 Roma tomatoes, quartered
1 red onion, sliced
100g feta cheese, crumbled
1–2 tablespoons finely shredded
basil leaves

9 sheets filo pastry, covered with damp
cloth to prevent drying out
olive oil spray
salt and freshly ground black pepper,
to serve
extra basil leaves, to garnish

Preheat grill. Grill capsicums, skin up, on a greased baking tray until the skin blisters and blackens. Remove and cover with paper or plastic for 5 minutes, then peel away the skin. Slice capsicums into thin strips.

Preheat oven to 200°C.

Place onions and tomatoes in a lightly greased baking dish and roast, uncovered, for about 30 minutes until onions have softened. Drain several times while roasting to remove as much liquid as possible.

Reduce oven to 190°C.

Gently combine capsicums, tomatoes, onion, feta and basil in a bowl. Lay 3 sheets of filo pastry on a flat, dry surface and spray top sheet with oil. Repeat process twice to create a stack of 9 sheets. Fold over edges to form 1cm border and transfer to a lined or greased baking tray. Spread vegetable mixture evenly over the shell, inside border. Bake for 15–20 minutes, until pastry is puffed and golden. Scatter with extra basil leaves and serve.

Note: This recipe can also be prepared as individual tarts by lining muffin tins with filo.
(SERVES 4–6)

~

Watermelon Salad

1 medium seedless watermelon
1 small white onion, very finely sliced
1 tablespoon fresh mint, finely chopped

Remove the skin and any seeds from the watermelon and cut into 2cm cubes.

Toss watermelon and onion lightly together in a large bowl and chill well. Sprinkle with fresh mint before serving.
(SERVES 8–10)

Snow Pea & Pear Salad

15–20 snow peas, trimmed
½ iceberg lettuce
60g baby rocket leaves
½ small red onion, finely sliced
8 baby beetroots (tinned), drained and
   cut in half
2 pears unpeeled (beurre bosc, nashi
   or corella)
feta cheese or blue vein cheese,
   crumbled for garnish (optional)
½ cup walnuts, roughly chopped

GINGER DRESSING

2 tablespoons white wine vinegar
1 tablespoon olive oil
1 tablespoon light soy sauce
1 teaspoon grated ginger
1 teaspoon lemon zest
2 teaspoons honey
salt and freshly ground black pepper,
   to taste

Make dressing: Place all ingredients in a screw-top jar and shake well.

Blanch the snow peas in boiling water for a few seconds, drain and place them into ice-cold water and drain again. This will retain the bright green colour.

Place lettuce, rocket, onion, beetroot and snow peas on a salad platter. Core and slice pears and place on top. Pour over dressing and garnish with cheese and walnuts.

(SERVES 6–8)

~

Viennese Cucumber Salad

6 firm large Lebanese cucumbers or
   3 small Telegraph cucumbers
1–2 tablespoons salt

DRESSING

½ cup white vinegar
2–3 tablespoons sugar or equivalent
artificial powdered sweetener
2 teaspoons white pepper
¼ cup cold water

Make dressing: Place all ingredients in a screw-top jar and shake well.

Peel the cucumbers and slice finely using the slicing side of an upright grater or a mandolin. The sliced rounds need to be almost transparent. Place the cucumbers in a small bowl, so that they almost reach the top. Stir through the salt and place a plate or wide bowl on top to press the cucumbers down. (The salt and pressure will release the excess liquid from the cucumbers.) Cover tightly with plastic wrap and refrigerate for at least 2 hours. Drain the liquid from the cucumbers. Pour over dressing and gently stir through.

(SERVES 6)

Truffled Polenta *Shannon Bennett's recipe, courtesy of the Gillian Helfgott*

1 tablespoon extra virgin olive oil

1 brown onion, finely grated

1 clove garlic, crushed

2 vegetable stock cubes,
dissolved in 1 litre boiling water

200g instant polenta

50ml red wine vinegar

5ml truffle oil

150g unsalted butter

salt and freshly ground black
pepper, to taste

50g parmesan, grated

Heat a frying pan and add oil. Fry the onions and garlic over a low heat until translucent. Add vegetable stock and bring to the boil. Slowly rain the polenta in, whisking constantly. Return to the boil and remove from heat. Stir in the vinegar, truffle oil, butter, salt and pepper and whisk very well; the consistency should be like porridge. Sprinkle with parmesan and serve as an accompaniment to fish or as a vegetarian dish with salad. (SERVES 8)

~

Tasty Tomato Recipes

Caramelised Onions & Tomatoes

6 tablespoons extra virgin olive oil

4 large red onions, peeled, quartered
and finely sliced

½ tablespoon dried oregano or
1 tablespoon finely chopped fresh
oregano

1 clove garlic, crushed

salt and freshly ground black pepper, to
taste

1 teaspoon sugar

6–8 ripe Roma tomatoes, cut into chunks

Heat olive oil in a large fry pan over medium-low heat. Add onions and cook until they begin to brown. Add oregano, garlic, salt, pepper and sugar and continue to cook for about 30 minutes, stirring occasionally until the mixture is very soft and lightly caramelised. Add more oil, if it starts to stick. Gently stir in tomatoes and continue to simmer until tomato juices have evaporated.
(SERVES 6)

Tomatoes Provençale

4 firm medium-sized ripe tomatoes
2 tablespoons butter
1 clove garlic, crushed
½ teaspoon salt

4 tablespoons breadcrumbs
½ cup finely grated extra tasty/sharp
   cheese
freshly ground pepper

Preheat the grill. Line a baking tray with baking paper or foil and lightly grease. Cut tomatoes crossways into halves and place on the baking tray. Melt butter in a small pan and stir through garlic and salt. Remove from heat before it turns brown. Add breadcrumbs, mix well and stir through grated cheese. Divide and spoon mixture equally over the top of the tomatoes and place under grill until golden. Sprinkle with pepper and serve hot.

(SERVES 4)

~

Roasted Truss Tomatoes

500g vine-ripened baby truss tomatoes
1 tablespoon balsamic vinegar
1 teaspoon olive oil

Preheat oven to 220°C. Combine all ingredients and place in a shallow baking dish. Roast uncovered for 10 minutes.

(SERVES 4)

Bagel Toppings

Anchovy Spread

1 x 80g tin/jar anchovy fillets in oil, drained
1 tablespoon milk
2 tablespoon unsalted butter, at room temperature

Soak anchovies in milk for 30 minutes. Drain on paper towels and pat dry. Chop finely and mix through softened butter. Spoon into a serving bowl or ramekin. (Mixture may be refrigerated up to 5 days.)

~

Liptauer Spread

250g Philadelphia cream cheese or
    substitute, softened at room
    temperature
a little milk
1 small white onion, finely grated
2 teaspoons mustard, French or German

½ teaspoon caraway seeds
    (optional)
1 teaspoon sweet paprika
extra paprika to garnish

Mix cream cheese with a little milk until really creamy. Thoroughly stir through remaining ingredients. The spread should have a slightly rose colour. Spoon into serving bowl or ramekin and refrigerate. To garnish, sprinkle gently with paprika.

Crunchy Cabbage Salad with Lemon Dressing

1 small Chinese cabbage, finely shredded
3–4 spring onions, thinly sliced
1 cup bean sprouts
2 tablespoons flat-leaf parsley, chopped
1 tablespoon dill, chopped
½ cup raw pepitas
½ cup sunflower seeds

LEMON DRESSING
2 lemons, juiced
1 clove garlic, crushed
3 tablespoons caster sugar
4 tablespoons olive oil
salt and freshly ground black pepper,
   to taste

Make lemon dressing: Combine all ingredients in a jug and whisk until creamy. Set aside.

Make salad: Combine cabbage, spring onions, bean sprouts, parsley and dill in a large bowl. When ready to serve, pour dressing over salad, toss gently and sprinkle with seeds.

Note: If fresh dill is unavailable use ½ tablespoon dried dill.

(SERVES 8)

Something Substantial

- Ghormeh Sabzi: Persian Lamb with Herbs
- Bin-Bin Chicken
- Chicken Fricassée
- Cointreau Fillets of Duck
- Salt 'n' Pepper Crusted Beef
- Quick Pan-Fried Fish with Saffron-Infused Tahina Sauce
- Baked Fish à la Dudu
- Pomegrante Ahsh
- Aromatic Roast Brisket
- Salmon Fillets with Green Peppercorn, Mushroom & Macadamia Nut Sauce
- Blazing Hot Wing Sauce with Beer
- Aussie-Style Blazing Hot Wing Sauce with Beer
- Marinated Fresh Tuna Kebabs
- Salade Niçoise with Smoked Trout or Peppered Mackerel
- Fresh Trout Fettuccine
- Exotic Chilli-Lime Fish Parcels
- BBQ Chicken with Zesty Sauce
- Barbecue Chicken Fillets with Chilli Mango Salsa
- Chicken Pearl; Sweet Chilli & Balsamic Chicken
- Osso Bucco
- G'Roestl Leftovers
- Bondi Steak Sandwich
- Gingered Thai Beef Salad
- Lettuce Delights
- Waldorf Turkey Salad
- Veal in White Wine with Tarragon
- Veal Piccante
- Veal Tenderloins

Rabbi Shmuley Boteach is an internationally acclaimed author, speaker and media personality.

RABBI SHMULEY BOTEACH

He was born in 1966 in Los Angeles to Yoav and Eleanor.

After completing rabbinical studies in Australia, Israel and the United States, Shmuley moved to Oxford University at age 21 to become the residential rabbi. He established the L'Chaim Society which became the second-largest student organisation in Oxford's history. During his eleven years at Oxford he interviewed many world leaders and celebrities including Mikhail Gorbachev, Shimon Peres, Michael Jackson and Deepak Chopra.

Rabbi Shmuley is the author of over eighteen books, many of which have been widely translated, that encompass issues on relationships and sexuality, racism, gender equality, G-d and human suffering. His bestsellers include *Kosher Sex, Dating Secrets of the Ten Commandments, Hating Women: America's Hostile Campaign Against the Fairer Sex, 10 Conversations You Need to Have With Your Children* and *The Broken American Male: And How to Fix Him*.

In 1999, Rabbi Shmuley was the first-ever Jewish winner of the highly prestigious London Times Preacher of the Year award in London. He has featured in many of the world's leading publications such as *Time* magazine, the *Washington Post* and other journals around America, and is a weekly columnist for the *Jerusalem Post*. In 2005, Rabbi Shmuley won the American Jewish Press Association's highest award for excellence in commentary. He hosts the national television show *Shalom in the Home,* which debuted in 2006.

Rabbi Shmuley is married to his Australian-born wife Debbie. They have eight children and currently live in Englewood, New Jersey, USA.

That's Not Kosher!

I was once invited to appear as a guest chef on a television show in Great Britain. The show was presenting a segment on kosher cuisine. I laughed because I can't cook.

My father is from Iran so I decided to make one of his favourite Persian dishes called *Ghormeh Sabzi*. Knowing my predicament, my wife offered to help. 'I'll prepare one for you at home and then tell you how it's made and you'll be able to demonstrate it.' The program was filmed in a perfect studio kitchen in London. *Baruch HaShem*, Thank G-d, it wasn't live. It was just so comical because I had no clue what I was doing and I mixed and added and cooked until it caught fire. And still, this concoction had to be presented as a gourmet kosher dish!

I had to taste my own creation and pretend while smiling for the camera. Through my grin, I thought, 'This is truly disgusting. I'm too young to die!' People watching the show would have got the impression that this was typical of kosher food – charred black and fried to a crisp. I really felt sorry for the poor crew member who unwittingly tasted this dish. For the sake of the Jewish people I decided against any further cooking adventures.

~

Travelling by plane when you only eat kosher can be a problem. I was flying with my father from Miami to Los Angeles after my nephew's ritual circumcision. The main meal at the celebration or *simcha* had been duck and the caterer had given my father a doggie bag – an entire duck to take home. We boarded the plane. No kosher food. My father smiled and turned to me, 'We can eat duck!'

'How can we possibly eat duck?' I replied, 'We have no knives, no forks, nothing.'

My father simply ripped the poor duck apart with his bare hands, limb by limb. Every passenger stared at us. Ducks are particularly fatty and my father's hands were covered in grease. He tried to tempt his hungry son to eat but I had lost my appetite and graciously declined with, 'I think I can survive on Coca-Cola until we land.'

~

When I was a child I had an aversion to meat because I couldn't imagine eating something that had been alive. My mother convinced me that meat grew on trees and whenever I ate it, I said, 'Mom, how do you soften the bark?' and she would say, 'I marinate it, and soak it in water until it is soft.' So for the first few years of my life, I thought that when eating steak I was eating something straight from a tree. It even looked like tree bark!

Ghormeh Sabzi: Persian Lamb with Herbs

Full of flavour

⅓ cup of olive oil
1 large onion, finely chopped
1 teaspoon ground turmeric
2–3 cloves garlic, crushed
1kg trim lamb, cubed
1½ cups water
¾ cup tinned kidney beans, rinsed and
    drained
salt and freshly ground black pepper,
    to taste

1 large potato, cubed
1 cup spring onions, finely chopped
½ cup flat-leaf parsley, finely chopped
¼ cup fresh coriander, finely chopped
½ cup lime juice
1½ cups spinach (or baby spinach
    leaves), finely chopped

Heat half the oil in a large saucepan and fry onions and garlic over low heat, until golden. Increase the heat, add turmeric and lamb cubes, searing meat on all sides until nicely browned. Reduce heat and add water, kidney beans, salt and pepper. Cover and simmer for 1–1½ hours, until meat is tender.

While the meat is cooking, heat remaining oil in a pan and fry potatoes until just cooked and lightly browned. Remove from heat.

When the meat is cooked, stir through potatoes, spring onions and herbs. Reheat, stir through lime juice and spinach until it just begins to wilt but remains green. Adjust seasoning. Serve with steamed white rice.

(SERVES 6)

Bella Italy — La dolce Vita

NESHAMA CARLEBACH

Neshama Carlebach is a singer and songwriter.

Born in New York, she is the eldest daughter of the late Rabbi Shlomo Carlebach, of blessed memory, and Rebbitzin Neila Carlebach.

Continuing in the tradition of her late father, Neshama brings her Jewish spirit to her singing and storytelling. People of all ages enjoy her genre of jazz/pop Jewish soul music, and she performs throughout the US, Canada, Europe and Israel.

As described in the *Jewish Book Mall:* 'Neshama is a miracle because she is outside of the realm of the ordinary. She brings more light into the world whenever she sings. Like pulling down a little bit of heaven, to enjoy so sweetly here on earth. It doesn't matter how observant you are – it doesn't even matter if you are Jewish – what matters is that you open your heart when you listen to her music and her father's music, and allow yourself to be blessed by it.'

In 2002, Neshama received an award from the City of New York for her accomplishments in Jewish music and contributions to the Jewish community.

Neshama and her husband Steven Katchen currently live in New York. They have one son.

'No pork! No shrimp! How can I make Chinese food without shrimp?'

Not so long ago, my sister Dari found a bottle of Chinese cough syrup. One sniff and childhood memories came flooding back.

I grew up in Canada with a Chinese nanny, which was very unusual at the time. Her name was Bin-Bin and she was a real intellectual as well as being a very special woman. She came to Canada to study for a PhD and to learn about another culture. Her father had been the head of economics and her mother the head of Japanese studies at Beijing University. Bin-Bin always said that Mao stole ten years of her life; the family was no longer allowed to teach or study, their home was closed down and she and her siblings sent to work as peasants in the country. Bin-Bin worked cultivating rice in the fields and cooked for the workers and the family with whom she boarded.

In Canada, Bin-Bin had a student visa which did not allow her to work. When my mother advertised for a new nanny for my sister and me, Bin-Bin answered the ad. She had tired of her studies and wanted to extend her stay in Canada. My mother lobbied our local member of parliament and Bin-Bin was awarded a work visa. She lived with us for four years, and they were indeed eventful years.

I clearly remember when Bin-Bin began cooking our *Shabbat* meals. My mother taught her to make chicken soup and it turned out to be an incredible combination of the Oriental and the kosher. We would sit in the kitchen, watch and listen to her complain, half in jest, 'No pork! No shrimp! How can I make Chinese food without shrimp?' And yet, Bin-Bin's kosher creations using mere chicken and fish became Chinese stir-fry delicacies. We knew she added the usual corn starch, soy sauce and garlic but when, out of the corner of her eye, she would see us watching her every move, she would quickly turn around to put in her secret spices. She would bend her head ever so slightly, cover her mouth and giggle.

Bin-Bin would give her dishes original names such as 'Chicken Chicken', 'Chicken Radish' and 'Red Fish'. She was always upset about not having her usual ingredients and would say with distaste, 'Food look like old lady feet', referring to the old Chinese tradition of binding women's feet.

We learned so much about her Chinese culture. My name, Neshama, translated from Hebrew means 'soul' and my sister's name, Nedara, means 'promise'. Bin-Bin would call us Ling Hwan and Si Wong, the Chinese equivalents.

Bin-Bin would tell us charming children's stories, like 'Three Hair Boy', and would often sing to us in Chinese. We learned her melodies and lyrics thinking we

above: Neshama singing with her band.

right: Neshama with her late father, Rabbi Shlomo Carlebach.

ONE EGG IS A FORTUNE

were singing beautiful love songs but in fact they would be about a slug climbing a flower, or a rejected lover sadly descending a mountain. On Shabbat we would sing our Hebrew songs and then the Chinese ones she'd taught us. My mother and father were an appreciative audience.

Bin-Bin's sense of humour always made us laugh. To guests she would say thing like, 'The lines on your face are very beautiful' or, 'Maybe you live long or maybe you die soon.'

Bin-Bin was a joy – she entertained us, she cooked for us, and she loved us. And we loved her. We all feel very blessed to have known Bin-Bin. She added that little bit of extra magic that enriched our lives.

I clearly remember when Bin-Bin began cooking our Shabbat meals. My mother taught her to make chicken soup and it turned out to be an incredible combination of the Oriental and the kosher.

Bin-Bin Chicken

Asian flavours

4 tablespoons honey
½ cup soy sauce
½ cup lemon juice
2 tablespoons sesame oil
2 onions, roughly chopped
4 skinless chicken breasts, sliced
   into strips
500g assorted green vegetables, such
   as snow peas, French green beans,
   asparagus

1 red capsicum, sliced into strips
¾ cup roasted unsalted cashews
1 small hot red chilli, seeded and
   sliced (reserving a little for garnish)
¼ cup fresh coriander leaves, chopped
   (reserving a little for garnish)

Make sauce: Whisk together honey, soy sauce and lemon juice.

Make stir-fry: Place a large frying pan or wok on high heat. Add oil and onions and cook for 2 minutes, remove from pan and set aside.

Stir-fry chicken strips in small batches, so as not to stew, until golden brown. Add all vegetables to the wok, stir-frying for a few minutes. As the colour changes, stir through the honey, soy sauce and lemon juice.

Add the chicken to reheat. Stir through chilli, coriander and cashews and garnish. Serve with steamed rice or noodles.

(SERVES 4)

PHYLLIS CHESLER

Phyllis Chesler is an emerita professor of psychology and women's studies, a leading feminist psychologist, a psychotherapist, and a renowned expert courtroom witness.

Phyllis was born in 1940 in New York State to Leon (Arye Leib) and Lillian Faige Leah (D'vora) and grew up in Brooklyn. Her paternal grandfather immigrated to America from Russia before World War I and her maternal grandparents from Poland in the early twentieth century.

Phyllis is the author of hundreds of articles and thirteen books including the bestselling and influential *Women and Madness*. Her latest books include *Woman's Inhumanity to Woman, Women on the Wall: Claiming Sacred Ground at Judaism's Holy Site, The New Anti-Semitism: The Current Crisis and What We Must Do About It,* and *The Death of Feminism: What's Next in the Struggle for Women's Freedom.* She continues to lecture and organise political, legal, religious and human rights campaigns worldwide, often speaking to medical, feminist, interfaith and Jewish groups.

Phyllis has lived in Afghanistan and Israel. She now lives in Manhattan near her son and daughter-in-law.

Unforgettable Food

W hen my father was an infant in Lutzk, Cossacks slaughtered his mother for whom I am named. His grandfather managed to save him and send him to his other grandfather who had already reached safety in America. My father struggled to earn his living: he was once a short-order cook, a long-distance trailer-truck driver, and even briefly, a cowboy.

What he cooked was very simple, but he did it with such relish and seriousness, and it was so delicious, that I have never forgotten it. Nor have I tasted anything quite like it again.

His most memorable dish was chopped eggs and onions for which he used chicken fat and salted it until it glowed on your tongue. Sometimes he would get a terrible headache as he cut up the onions and I remember him donning a headache-headband which, in retrospect, made him look like a sushi chef!

My mother's special dish was chicken fricassée. The sauce was so rich, so brown, so deep and so onion-flavoured that I have never tasted its like again.

On long hot summer days my curfew would be extended and I would have many more hours of daylight in which to read or sit outside. My mother would prepare a cooling dish, a spring salad with cottage cheese or farmer-cheese and fresh radishes, tomatoes, celery and cucumbers.

I wish I had these exact recipes but as I was a book addict back then, I would have nothing to do with kitchen chores. I'd recognise these dishes again instantly and fully expect to do so in the Next World! (If one actually eats there, which is doubtful, but possible.)

Chicken Fricassée
Comfort food

12 small chicken drumsticks
1 cup plain flour
1 tablespoon sweet paprika
½ tablespoon salt
½ tablespoon freshly ground black
   pepper
½ cup oil
2 cups onions, diced
1 cup celery, diced
2 large cloves garlic, crushed

1 stock cube, dissolved in 2 cups hot water
½ cup white wine
12 baby carrots, peeled
12 baby potatoes, peeled
¼ cup finely sliced spring onions
½ cup finely chopped flat-leaf parsley
extra salt, freshly ground black pepper,
   to taste
Tabasco sauce (optional)

Place ½ cup flour, paprika, salt, pepper and chicken in a bag and shake well. Refrigerate for 1 hour to allow seasoned flour to stick.

Heat ¼ cup oil in a large saucepan. Fry chicken pieces, a few at a time, until golden brown on all sides, remove and set aside.

Sauté onions, celery and garlic in the same pan, until onions turn translucent and set aside. Add remaining oil to same saucepan, whisk in remaining flour and stir until golden brown. Add stock and wine, a little at a time, stirring until all lumps have disappeared and the sauce is thick and smooth.

Place the pan-fried chicken, sautéed vegetables, carrots and potatoes in the sauce and bring to the boil. Reduce heat, cover and simmer for 45 minutes or until chicken is tender. Add extra water if sauce becomes too thick. When ready to serve, stir in spring onions, parsley and season with extra salt, pepper and Tabasco.

Accompany with steamed white rice, small pasta or dumplings.
(SERVES 6)

Alan Crown AM
was an emeritus
professor,
academic, author
and international
expert on the Dead
Sea Scrolls and the
Samaritans.

ALAN CROWN

He was born in Leeds, UK, in 1932, the son of Abraham and Sarah. From 1955–57, Alan served as a sergeant instructor in the Royal Army Educational Corps and then worked as a schoolmaster in Leeds. In 1959, he moved to Australia with his wife Sadie and children Jacqui and Aviva.

Alan took up a position in the Semitic studies department of Sydney University and completed a PhD there in 1967. He became the administrator of the International Dead Sea Scrolls Program for the Oxford Centre for Hebrew and Jewish Studies. He was a visiting professor at international universities, including UCLA and London.

Alan's love of facilitating Jewish education led to his involvement in the establishment of Mandelbaum House, a Jewish residential college at Sydney University, where he was a trustee and joint honorary master and chairman of council. He also had a personal chair in Hebrew, Bible and Jewish studies at Sydney University. He was a founding project director of the *Archive of Australian Judaica* and wrote numerous articles and papers and lectured widely. His other areas of expertise included Jewish education, Australian Jewry, the Samaritans and Zionism.

In 1994 Alan received the Jewish Continuity Award for his contribution to the promotion, advancement and development of the Jewish community of NSW. In 1995 he was appointed a Member of the Order of Australia in the General Division in recognition of his services to education, particularly in the field of Semitic studies.

Alan made his home in Sydney with his wife, two children and six grandchildren. Sadly, he passed away in November 2010.

There is a Story in Every Life Experience

When I was a geography teacher I became acquainted with the old fellow who runs the ruins at the Whitby Abbey near Roxby, overlooking the wild North Yorkshire coast. I gained permission to take my students up there to have some fun when teaching map-reading. This excursion involved camping and was a highlight of the course. My students knew that if they played up during class, they would be excluded. My wife used to accompany the group, bake a cake or bring a big hamper of food which included a huge roasted piece of meat. The kids loved it!

~

We immigrated to Australia in 1959 and first settled in Melbourne. I was teaching at Mount Scopus College and my wife was employed as an illustrator at Melbourne University. The poor girl used to come home so late. I knew it was unfair for her and my daughters to do all the cooking so I decided to help out. One of my favourite foods was *gefilte* fish so I rang my wife at work for the recipe. Surprised that this was my choice for dinner, she listed the ingredients and explained how to prepare the dish.

I started cooking. Everything seemed to go according to plan. I felt so pleased with myself. But something went horribly wrong and we ended up with *gefilte* fish bisque for dinner. Why? My wife had omitted one small but crucial detail: to place the prepared raw fish balls into boiling water and I, unfortunately, had been so very clever and put them in cold water. This was one of the recipes I learnt very quickly.

~

We did not know anyone when we moved to Sydney in 1962. We were living in Kings Cross and would chat to the tourists at a nearby hotel. I remember starting a conversation with an Israeli fellow. 'I've only just arrived,' I said, 'and I don't know anybody. I've been here two months.' He could not understand this. 'Well, that's ridiculous,' he said. 'You've got to find ways of meeting people. Why don't you get involved in the Friends of the Hebrew University of Jerusalem? I will introduce you to some of my friends.'

This was a turning point in our lives. After four months I was on the committee and within six months, I was president. From not knowing anybody, now we were acquainted with hundreds and hundreds of people. We started having regular dinner parties and my culinary skills were put to the test; one of my house specialities became duck, and I became the resident chef.

Cointreau Fillets of Duck

A dinner party favourite

2 oranges

1 extra orange, juiced

1 tablespoon lemon juice

1 tablespoon caster sugar

1 tablespoon cornflour (potato flour may be substituted)

3 tablespoons cold tap water

6 skinless duck breasts (chicken may be substituted)

20g margarine

2 tablespoons Cointreau or other orange-flavoured liqueur

Make garnish: Using a small sharp paring knife, remove the rind and white pith from the oranges. Slice the rind from 1 orange into long, thin strips and remove white bitter pith and set aside. Carefully cut the oranges into segments, remove any remaining pith and set aside.

Make sauce: This can be prepared ahead or whilst the duck is cooking. Pour orange juice, lemon juice and sugar into a saucepan and gently heat. When sugar has dissolved, remove from heat. Combine cornflour and cold tap water. Add into the juices, stir until smooth and set aside.

Make fillets: Slice the breasts lengthwise into two equal halves. Melt the margarine and pan-fry fillets until golden.

Stirring constantly, reheat the sauce until just beginning to boil and add the Cointreau. Arrange fillets on plates, top with orange segments, pour sauce over and garnish with orange strips. Serve immediately.

(SERVES 6)

ALAN DERSHOWITZ

Alan Dershowitz is an academic and human rights lawyer.

He was born in Brooklyn, New York, in September 1938 to Harry and Claire Dershowitz. Growing up in Borough Park, Alan attended Yeshiva University High School and in 1959 received a Bachelor of Arts degree from Brooklyn College. He furthered his studies at Yale Law School and in 1962 graduated first in his class. During this time Alan served as editor-in-chief of the *Yale Law Journal*.

At the age of 28, Alan became Harvard Law School's youngest full professor of law. He continued to work at Harvard and later became the Felix Frankfurter Professor of Law. Alan has taught many courses, including criminal law, psychiatry and law, constitutional litigation, civil liberties and violence, neurobiology and the law, and a collaborative philosophy course. He is renowned for his legal acumen and has been involved in many contentious high-profile legal cases.

As a fervent supporter of Israel, Alan comments regularly on issues related to Judaism, Israel, civil rights and the War on Terror. He has been an active member of the American Civil Liberties Union and the Anti-Defamation League of B'nai B'rith. He makes frequent media and public appearances and lectures around the world.

His many honorary degrees and medals are testament to his contribution to society.

In 1979 Alan was awarded a Guggenheim Fellowship for his work in human rights. He is also a prolific author and has written more than 24 books including *The Case for Peace: How the Arab–Israeli Conflict Can be Resolved* and *The Case for Israel*.

Alan is married to Carolyn Cohen, a psychologist, and they currently live in Massachusetts. They have three children.

One Person's Prison Food is Another's Delicacy

In the 1970s I spent much of my time representing Jewish dissidents from the Soviet Union. Silva (Sylva) Zalmonson was one such person. She was born in Riga in the former Soviet Union in 1944 and protested against the USSR's treatment of Jews. In 1970 she attempted to defect to Israel but was detained in a gulag, a forced labour camp for political prisoners, with her husband and a number of other lawyers. I helped to secure her freedom.

We met her at the airport; she had literally been flown from the gulag to the United States. During her trip from the airport to downtown New York, Silva said that since she'd been in the gulag for such a long time, all she really wanted was a good old-fashioned Jewish meal. We arranged to take her to a kosher restaurant in midtown New York called Lou G. Segal's. This restaurant, located in the heart of the garment district, was famous for its traditional Jewish food. I telephoned ahead and spoke to the owner, Mr. Lou G. Segal. I explained that our guest had specifically requested a really, really special meal.

The first dish to arrive was a steaming bowl of *cholent*. It smelled fantastic, it looked fantastic, and I myself was dying to dig into it. But, of course, Silva was the guest of honour and she had to start. She stared and stared at it. She picked up a fork, stuck it into the *cholent*, tasted it and spat it out, yelling 'Pfah!'

In surprise I asked, 'What's the matter? You asked for Jewish food.'

'This is not Jewish food, this is prison food! They have been feeding me this for the last several years,' she exclaimed.

And what is *cholent*? *Cholent* is a very inexpensive food – potatoes, beans and tiny bits of meat just enough for flavour. To my disappointment, the waiters took the dish away.

I suddenly realised that the concept of traditional Jewish food is a cultural perception and differs from place to place. As our families had come from Russia, Poland or other parts of Europe where they were poor and food was scarce, they had made the most of the little scraps they had. Wherever they settled they cooked the meals they knew and over time these became delicacies to be savoured. So what we thought was Jewish food was prison food to another!

'I heard that the good Jewish dish in America is something called rare roast beef,' said Silva. We were dumbfounded. That is as Jewish as you can get! Silva had no interest in *kneidlach*[1], *kreplach*[2] or *kishke*[3] – this was all peasant food to her. We called the waiter and ordered rare roast beef and steak. She absolutely relished the meal. This was Silva's introduction to American Jewish food.

1   Dumplings made from crushed matzo, the unleavened bread eaten at Passover.
2   Dumplings filled with ground meat, similar to ravioli, boiled and served in chicken soup.
3   Beef casings filled with meat, onions, vegetables, chicken fat, boiled and then roasted.

Salt 'n' Pepper Crusted Beef

Explosion of taste

200g crushed sea salt

3 tablespoons freshly ground mixed peppercorn medley

6 pieces Scotch fillet of beef

olive oil

extra sea salt

mustard or horseradish

Mix salt and pepper and spread it evenly over a flat tray to form a thick layer and set aside.

Heat non-stick fry pan until very hot, add a little oil and brown both sides of the meat. Gently place each piece of beef onto the tray, coat each side well and allow to rest for 10 minutes.

Heat the fry pan again and cook each fillet for a further 2 minutes on each side. Drizzle with olive oil and sprinkle with extra sea salt.

Serve accompanied with mustard or horseradish.

(SERVES 6)

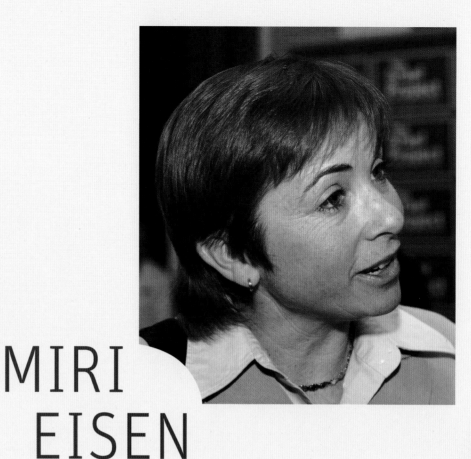

MIRI EISEN

Miri Eisen is a retired Israel Defense Forces lieutenant-colonel and was a spokesperson for the foreign press for the former Israeli prime minister Ehud Olmert, the first female to hold this position.

Miri was born in 1962 in San Raphael, in northern California, to Morrie and Annette Bode. In 1971, the Eisen family, which included Miri and her two sisters Tova and Debbie, migrated to Israel.

Miri holds degrees in political science and Middle Eastern studies from Tel Aviv University and a Masters degree in security studies from Haifa University. She is also a graduate of the Israeli National Defense College and the Staff College. Miri has served over twenty years in the Israeli Defense Forces in army intelligence and as a special spokesperson for the Israeli government. She has also served as a special advisor to the Combined Jewish Philanthropies in Boston.

Miri lectures on subjects relating to her professional background. She is married to Gilad and they live in Israel with their three children.

My First Falafel

I was a hamburger, French fries, peanut butter and jelly girl from California. After a three-week holiday to Israel, my parents decided to make *aliyah*, establishing our new home in Israel, when I finished third grade. We spent our first six months in an absorption centre learning Hebrew. Moving from northern California to the small town of Afula was a little extreme. Apart from the intense culture shock, the drastic change was the food – Israel has the best fresh vegetables but nine year-olds are notoriously against any kind!

The first time my sister and I took a bus into the centre of town, we went looking for a hamburger. We discovered that in Afula in 1971 there was no such thing. We returned home disappointed that Israel had only fresh tomatoes and cucumbers, and no fast food.

Our next outing into town was with our new Israeli friends from the absorption centre – immigrants from the USSR, Morocco and Iran. We all went looking for food. I wanted a hamburger. My Russian friend wanted smoked herring. My Moroccan friend wanted couscous, and my Iranian friend wanted to eat stuffed eggplant. We were four nine year-olds, each on a personal quest to find food from our previous life.

The summer was hot and dry, and the bus took us from the absorption centre to the central bus station. As the kiosk only offered candy and snacks, we left the station and walked to the main square. We looked around and saw signs in Hebrew. Although all four of us had learned to read Hebrew, no one was yet fluent. It was obvious that the food we wanted was not offered. But something smelt so good! We could see a line of people at a stand waiting to be served. They were eating with their hands. We figured, what could be bad about finger food? Between the four of us we understood that the food was called falafel. We took a deep breath and asked for a falafel each. We were bombarded with a series of questions that no one understood and we reverted to using the pointing method. In pita or lafa? With tahina or hummus? With salad or French fries? With spicy sauce or without? I chose non-spicy with French fries. We found a bench in the shade and took our first bite into our new food. We discovered that every country has their own great fast food – who needs hamburgers?

I still live in Israel, and my favourite food is still a good falafel. What still amazes me is how cheap it is – and how satisfying!

Today I still stop in Afula at my first falafel stand and enjoy a bite, remembering how four nine year-olds discovered the taste of their new country.

Quick Pan-Fried Fish with Saffron-Infused Tahina Sauce

Deliciously simple

6 x 200g white fish fillets, skinned and
   pin-boned
plain flour, for dusting
2–3 tablespoons olive oil
2–3 tablespoons unsalted butter
salt and freshly ground black pepper,
   to taste
2 tablespoons sesame seeds
2 tablespoons fresh flat-leaf parsley,
   finely chopped
6 lemon wedges

SAFFRON-INFUSED TAHINA SAUCE
8 tablespoons ready-prepared tahina
¼ cup lemon juice
saffron threads, a pinch soaked in ½ cup
   warm water

Make sauce: Toast sesame seeds in a dry frying pan until light brown and fragrant (watch closely as they burn easily). Combine tahina and lemon juice in a jug and gently mix in saffron threads and water.

   Make fish: Add salt and pepper to the flour and dust fish liberally, shaking off excess. Heat the oil and butter in a non-stick fry pan and gently fry fish until cooked through and golden on both sides. Place fillets on individual plates and spoon a generous amount of sauce over the top. Garnish with sesame seeds, parsley and lemon wedges.
(SERVES 6)

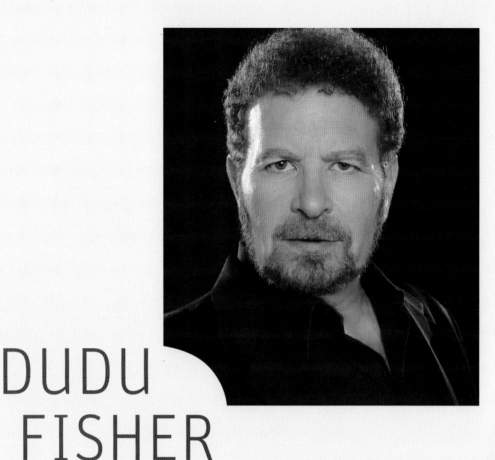

DUDU FISHER

Dudu (David) Fisher is a talented and versatile Israeli cantor and stage performer.

He travels the world singing different genres of music, from traditional Chassidic/Yiddish to Broadway musicals, and is renowned for his performances as Jean Valjean in the musical *Les Misérables*.

Dudu was born in 1952 in Petach Tikvah, Israel. Following three years of military service during which he kept the troops entertained, he studied with legendary cantors and at the Tel Aviv Academy of Music. At the age of 22, Dudu accepted the position of cantor at the Great Synagogue of Tel Aviv. He has been invited to work as a cantor all over the world.

Dudu saw his first live musical *Les Misérables* in London in 1986. This compelled him to audition for a forthcoming Israeli production in Hebrew, even though he had no theatre experience. The role of Jean Valjean catapulted Dudu into world stardom. He has performed for the British Royal Family, the Thai Royal Family, former president Bill Clinton, at Wembley Stadium for a World Cup soccer final, with the Israel Philharmonic Orchestra conducted by Zubin Mehta, on Broadway, and on London's West End. In 1989 Dudu was the first Israeli artist allowed to sing in Moscow. His religious observance has excused him from Friday night, Saturday matinees and all Jewish holy days. In his over thirty-year singing career, he has recorded more than twenty albums.

Dudu lives mainly in Tel Aviv. He is married with three adult children.

One Egg Equals a Fortune

Don't run, don't climb trees, don't play sport in case you hurt yourself ... just eat! That's the way I was brought up.

I was born 'David' but my grandmother Frieda called me Dudu, the Yiddish nickname. Having survived the Holocaust with virtually nothing to eat, she only wanted to see me as a fat little boy. When I was a small child aged four or five, I wasn't a big *fresser*, a Yiddish word for big eater. My grandmother never liked to see food left on a plate and so she would pay me for the food I ate. Grandmother Frieda designed a menu in her kitchen specifically for me. Each item of food had its own value and price-tag. For example, a piece of bread thickly spread with pure butter was worth ten *aggarot*, our smallest coin then, now about ½ shekel or ten cents; a large chunk of yellow cheese was an extra fifteen cents; sour cream was a further 25 cents and an egg a fortune.

One of her delicacies was pigeon soup, so much sweeter than chicken soup. I haven't had it for 45 years but I can still remember the taste. My grandfather Shmuel, the man who gave me my life and encouraged me to sing, was a *shochet*, a kosher butcher, and used to breed these pigeons.

My grandmother and I had developed a special relationship and I looked forward to visiting her, especially after school. 'Dudu, where are you going?' my mother would ask.

'To grandma's,' I would reply.

'Why?'

'I am going to have lunch there,' I said, thinking: why should I eat at home for free when I can earn pocket money simply by eating at grandma's?

Perhaps this is why I like to eat and I have struggled with my weight all my life. I love all kinds of food – Jewish food which is very heavy, Thai food which is spicy and French food because it is so tasty and expensive! My grandmother always insisted that I eat everything I was given, especially that last bite because it has all the energy.

Baked Fish à la Dudu

Sing for your supper

1 tablespoon olive oil

1 large white onion, thinly sliced

1kg freshwater fish fillets, such as carp,
barramundi or perch

salt and freshly ground pepper, to taste

2 large red or yellow capsicums,
thinly sliced

3 tomatoes, sliced

1 cup bottled Napoletana pasta sauce

¾ cup red wine

chives, finely chopped, for garnish

caperberries, for garnish (optional)

Preheat oven to 180°C. Heat olive oil in a non-stick fry pan and sauté onions until golden.

Place onions in an oiled baking dish and top with fish fillets. Season with salt and pepper. Cover fish with capsicums and tomatoes.

Combine pasta sauce and red wine and pour over the fish. Cover with foil and bake for 35–40 minutes until fish and capsicums are cooked.

Serve, garnished with chives and caperberries.

Note: This recipe also works well in a covered BBQ.

(SERVES 4–6)

GIL HOVAV

Gil Hovav is a leading culinary journalist and television personality in Israel.

He was born in 1962 in Jerusalem to Drora and Moshe Hovav and is the great-grandson of Eliezer Ben-Yehuda, credited as the reviver of modern Hebrew. After finishing school and serving four years in the intelligence division of the Israeli Defense Forces, Gil completed his studies in French and Arabic at the Hebrew University of Jerusalem.

Moving from a restaurant critic to a newspaper editor, Gil became involved in television. He created, produced and presented food shows including *Pepper, Garlic and Olive Oil, Captain Cook, Going to the Market* and *The Flying Chef*. Gil is looking forward to his new television series, *Food for Thought*, where he interviews Nobel Prize Laureates and cooks with them. He has his own production company, Toad Communications.

Gil has published three bestselling novels and many cookbooks, including those based on his television series. His new English book, *Confessions of a Kitchen Rebbetzin* will be released shortly. Gil's culinary repertoire has been influenced by his family ancestry from Israel, Yemen, north Africa and eastern Europe.

Gil travels the world lecturing and giving cooking demonstrations, combining personal stories with his knowledge of Israeli cuisine. His restaurant reviews are regularly broadcast on the radio.

Gil lives in Tel Aviv with his partner Danny and daughter Naomi.

Grandma Mouma Changes the Time

There is a German expression that says, 'There are people who fall into the pit that befits them.' I heard it from my German Freudian psychologist (one of many). It means that for some people, the things that need to happen do indeed occur, even though they are not smart enough to make them happen. (My psychologist did not think much of me). I can attest that this expression is correct. Look at me: I never wanted to be a writer. I never wanted to be a cook. And here I am – a writer and a television cook. I hate it when shrinks are right.

I cook (and write) in order to remember. Remember how much I was loved as a child, how wonderful my grandmother was, and what the mutual support of a family means. Our most important rule was that someone you love cannot be allowed to feel sad. My grandmother, who was not very rich, gave me a thousand gifts of love. She hugged, she believed, she made me laugh, she told stories and, most of all, she cooked. She could make magic in the kitchen that went far beyond cooking. She could shout at God and change the time and make the rain fall or the sun rise earlier, and she could even make a short cross-eyed child like me feel like a prince.

She never allowed me to help her in the kitchen. In the tradition she came from, men in the kitchen brought only two things: dirt and bad luck. When she died, she did not leave me any written recipes. I've reconstructed all of her dishes on my own, reinventing them solely from memory. I have an entire book of recipes that I reconstructed in this way. But to change time? That's something I'll never manage to do.

~

They never picked me when choosing sides for soccer. Usually I didn't care. I was too immersed in the red and frayed copy of Little Women, wondering whether Jo March would get married; or the green and tattered copy of 20,000 Leagues Under the Sea, trying to guess the real identity of Captain Nemo. Besides, it was clear to me that I had no chance: I was short, a four-eyes and a klutz. Why would anyone want to take a chance on me, even as a goalie?

But sometimes, when I didn't have a book, I would suddenly feel alone. I suddenly realised that they were on the field and I wasn't; that they were playing and I wasn't; that they were deciding what would happen and I – I was chasing submarines in the Indian Ocean. At times like these, I would return home despondent, grumpy and teary-eyed, and my grandmother Mouma would immediately mobilise to wage war against all my enemies.

'Don't cry 'kudillo' (sweetheart), don't shatter my heart,' she said to me. 'Why don't you go down to the garden and pick two beautiful fruits from the pomegranate tree we planted when you were born and bring them to me.'

Mouma's anger, which could sink a thousand submarines or marry off a hundred spinsters, raged in great waves at my friends from the soccer field, those who 'don't understand a thing, who will all grow up to be wagon-drivers and gamblers or I don't know what, and even without seeing them I can tell you they haven't washed their hair since Rosh Hashanah.' If her colorful tirade was still not enough to cheer me up, Mouma would pull from her arsenal of ammunition her greatest talent: Mouma could move time forward and backward, change the seasons of the year and switch the order of the days of the week. I'm not kidding. She didn't have money, but the forces of nature were at her beck and call.

'Don't cry *kudillo* (sweetheart), don't shatter my heart,' she said to me. 'Why don't you go down to the garden and pick two beautiful fruits from the pomegranate tree we planted when you were born and bring them to me.'

'But why?' I asked her. 'Explain to me why.' The pomegranates on our small and frail tree were considered a treasure and were only picked on Fridays, for preparing pomegranate *ahsh* – a meatball dish in thick, purple pomegranate sauce eaten only on the eve of Shabbat. So why all of a sudden pick them on a Wednesday?

'Don't drive me crazy with your questions, flea!' answered Mouma, who loved me but strictly held the balance of power in the kitchen. 'Do what I tell you and that's all. I already have enough work to do. And when you climb up the tree, be careful not to fall. You know that if you get hurt, or even get a scratch, I'll die here on the spot.'

Within an hour and a half, a steaming pot of *ahsh* was on the stove. Mouma served me a deep bowl of white rice (there was always a pot of white rice on the stove). She poured meatballs in purple sauce onto the rice, and piled a generous helping of fried onions on top. 'Eat *kudillo*, eat a lot. I knew you would like this dish and I prepared it especially for you. Do not be afraid to eat Friday food on Wednesday. If that's what it takes to make you smile, I'll arrange for it to be Friday seven days a week. Look how many pomegranates I put on the plate for you. They are full of iron and you'll see how they'll make you grow.'

'And I'll be a soccer player?' I asked.

'Heaven forbid! Nothing less than the ambassador to France. And the main thing is that you remember, *kudillo* – that you are a prince. Look at the pomegranates your tree produced. That tree is yours. Remember, we planted it on the day you were born. Look at them: there's a crown on the head of every pomegranate. There's a crown on your head too, do you understand? Maybe the rascals on the soccer field won't see it. But I see. I always see it and so, when you're here with me in the kitchen, for me it is always Friday. Here, I can already feel the scent of Shabbat. And it's all because of you, our prince. Promise me you'll remember that everything good in my world happened because of you. And now, don't drive me crazy with your questions. Get out of the kitchen, I have a week's worth of cooking to do. Out you go.'

Years have passed. Jo March got married. Captain Nemo turned out to be an Indian prince. I was not appointed ambassador to France. Mouma is no longer here for me and the house in Jerusalem, the one with the small and frail pomegranate tree in the backyard, was sold. But sometimes, when I'm feeling sad, I walk along the streets of Tel Aviv and peek into courtyards. And sometimes, if I'm lucky, I find a house with a pomegranate tree. I look at it and smile. And I remember.

Pomegranate Ahsh

Traditionally served on Fridays for lunch

This ahsh *is an old Persian dish of meatballs cooked in a rich, purple pomegranate broth. Do not try making it without fresh pomegranates. It brings bad luck.*

BROTH
2 cups chicken stock, fresh or made using 2 stock cubes dissolved in 2 cups boiling water
2 cups pomegranate juice
5 cups water
1 large lemon, juiced
3 cups mixed greens (dill, parsley, mint, coriander, celery leaves), finely chopped
2/3 cup long grain rice
2 beetroots, peeled and roughly chopped
12 spring onions, sliced
5 sticks celery, sliced
8 garlic cloves, peeled and chopped
2 cups pomegranate kernels

MEATBALLS
500g minced beef
1 egg
1 onion, finely chopped, juice squeezed out and discarded
2 garlic cloves, finely chopped
1 cup dill, finely chopped
2 tbsp breadcrumbs
1 tsp cumin
salt and pepper

GARNISH
2 onions, thinly sliced
oil, for frying

Make meatballs: Mix all ingredients and shape into balls slightly bigger than ping-pong balls. Cover and refrigerate for an hour.

Make broth: Add liquids to a large pot and bring to the boil. Add the rest of the ingredients and bring to the boil. Reduce heat, cover and cook for an hour, until the rice is tender and the broth begins to thicken. The meatballs are to be cooked in the broth in batches of three. Increase the heat, bring the broth to a boil and gently place three meatballs into the pot. When the broth begins to boil again, place another three meatballs into the pot. Repeat this process until all meatballs are in the broth. Cover and simmer for 30 minutes.

Make garnish: Heat the oil in a saucepan and fry onions until golden.

Serve meatballs with a little broth on white rice. Garnish with fried onions.

(SERVES 6-8)

SAM LIPSKI

Sam Lipski AM is an Australian journalist.

He was born in 1938 in Melbourne, Australia. His career as a print, radio and television journalist began in 1961 and he has worked in Australia, Israel, South East Asia, Europe and the United States where he was the first Washington correspondent for the *Australian*. Sam is a former editor-in-chief of the *Australian Jewish News* and continues to contribute regularly to the paper.

Since 1998 he has been the chief executive of the Pratt Foundation, the philanthropic trust of the Pratt family and the Visy Group of companies. From 2000–06 he was the president of the State Library of Victoria, and has continued to participate in a variety of advisory, community and voluntary organisations. He has received various awards, including radio's National News Commentator of the Year in 1982, a Member of the Order of Australia for services to the media in 1993, the Australian Centenary Medal for journalism in 2001, and an honorary Doctor of Laws from Monash University in 2008.

Sam is married to Aura Levin, has three children, and lives in Melbourne.

Flavours of Carlton

I'm a great food lover and I'm also the cook in our family. We have a division
of labour. My wife is a builder's daughter; she does all the house maintenance
work including the gardening, dealing with plumbers, electricians etc. ... I leave it
all up to her. But mostly I'm the cook. The trouble is I like my own food too much,
a very bad thing for a cook.

Many of my childhood memories are associated with food, made more vivid
because my late father Ezra was a talented and former professional cook. He'd
begun his working life in Poland as a chocolate manufacturer, and he had a sweet
tooth which unfortunately I inherited. On my father's side, going back many
hundreds of years, our family were wine and specialty food merchants. To the best
of our knowledge, we believe my father established the first Jewish restaurant in
Melbourne in 1927 called Café Tel Aviv after arriving from Poland via Palestine.
It was on the corner of Faraday and Drummond streets in Carlton, and to this day
it remains a restaurant. My father had the restaurant from 1927 to 1933. In later
years, my late mother Chana cooked but my father was always the chef.

I grew up in Carlton in the 1940s and '50s when the neighbourhood had a very
strong Jewish influence. The food stores were legendary – Poses's pickles, Monaco's
cake shop in Lygon Street, Bornstein's the grocer, and Polonsky's butchery. I
fondly remember buying a penny's worth of Mr Haber's broken biscuits wrapped
in a newspaper cone and eating them on the way to afternoon Hebrew school
in Rathdowne Street. In our home street, Drummond Street, we had Berland's
bakery. My father worked with Mr Berland during a bakery strike in the '40s when
Mr Berland was the only baker allowed to open on the north side of the Yarra. The
two of them didn't sleep for three days, baking rye bread around the clock, and
churning out thousands of the greatest onion rolls, the unforgettable *pletzlach*.

All the Jewish festivals evoke childhood food memories. The moment these
holidays begin I recall the smells and tastes of the *challahs* my father prepared at
home and baked in Mr Berland's ovens, as well as his wonderful honey cakes for
Rosh Hashanah and cheesecakes for *Shavuot*.

Quite simply, my father made the best cheesecake. *Ever.* Believe me when I say
I've tried cheesecake all over the world and I'm still in search of the perfect one.
Not one, anywhere – in Israel, the United States or in Australia – could compare to
my father's. Sadly I don't have his recipe.

Aromatic Roast Brisket
Not for the faint-hearted!

Fear not the 36–40 cloves of garlic! When roasted, garlic becomes sweet, nutty and delicious while losing much, though not quite all, of its pungency. This brisket is truly mouth-watering!

3 tablespoons olive oil
2kg lean piece beef brisket
salt and freshly ground pepper, to taste
3 tablespoons sweet paprika
36 cloves garlic (3–4 heads)

2 large onions, thinly sliced into rings
¼ cup red table wine
3 cups chicken/vegetable stock
¼ cup fresh coriander, chopped
¼ cup fresh flat-leaf parsley, chopped

The brisket can be cooked in a conventional oven or on a BBQ with a hood. This recipe requires a large heavy baking dish with a baking rack and tightly fitting lid. Alternatively, a large disposable aluminium-foil baking dish covered with foil can be used.

Preheat oven to 180°C or preheat a BBQ, hood closed.

Heat the baking dish. Add olive oil and sear both sides of brisket until golden. Remove to a plate and season brisket liberally on both sides with salt, pepper and paprika.

Add garlic and onion to the same unwashed baking dish and fry in the oil until garlic begins to turn golden and onion is soft. Add wine and stir until the 'browned bits' from frying are mixed through. Add stock, coriander and parsley and bring to the boil. Pour into a bowl and set aside. Insert the baking rack into the middle of the baking dish and place the brisket on top. Spoon garlic and onion mixture over the brisket, cover tightly, and place in the oven or on BBQ with hood closed. Roast brisket for 30 minutes, and baste with juices. Return to the oven for a further 30 minutes and baste again. When the meat is soft, remove from oven and allow to rest for 5–10 minutes.

Slice carefully across the meat's grain using a sharp knife and serve with the sauce from the pan.

(SERVES 8–10)

England — everyone's cup of tea

Dennis Ross is a scholar, diplomat and former United States ambassador with more than two decades' experience in Soviet and Middle East policy.

DENNIS
ROSS

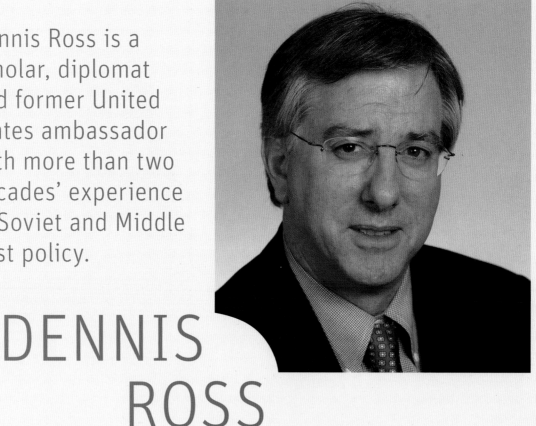

He was born in 1948, in San Francisco.

Dennis completed his undergraduate and graduate studies at the University of California with special emphasis on the USSR and the Middle East.

During the Reagan administration, Dennis served as director of Near East and South Asian Affairs on the National Security Council staff and as deputy director of the Pentagon's Office of Net Assessment. He served as director of the State Department's Policy Planning office in the first Bush administration, playing a prominent role in developing US policy toward the former Soviet Union, the unification of Germany, arms control negotiations, and the development of the 1991 Gulf War coalition.

Dennis played a leading role in the Middle East peace process under both the Bush Senior and Clinton administrations.

Former president Clinton awarded Dennis the Presidential Medal for Distinguished Federal Civilian Service, and former secretaries Baker and Albright presented him with the State Department's highest award. He has received UCLA's highest medal and has been named UCLA Alumni of the Year. He has also received honorary doctorates from the Jewish Theological Seminary, Amherst College and Syracuse University.

Dennis has published extensively and is the author of two books, *The Missing Peace: The Inside Story of the Fight for Middle East Peace* and *Statecraft: How to Restore America's Standing in the World*. He also writes for journals and newspapers.

As well as being a highly respected commentator on Middle East issues, Dennis has been a Counsellor and Ziegler Distinguished Fellow at the Washington Institute for Near East Policy. In 2009 Dennis was appointed as a Special Assistant and advisor to President Obama.

Dennis and his wife Deborah have three children and live in Washington, DC.

Good Diplomacy Works Well with Food

As a United States peace negotiator, I have been privileged to witness many remarkable events that have determined the course of history.

The United States played a major role in shaping the Middle East peace process and negotiated directly with all respective parties. In the fall of 1993, the then prime minister of Israel, Yitzhak Rabin, and the chairman of the Palestinian Liberation Organisation, Yasser Arafat, had shaken hands in the presence of president Bill Clinton and the cheering crowds. The public handshake on the White House lawn marked the signing of a Declaration of Principles for peace between the Arabs and Israelis. The PLO had agreed to end the intifada and terrorist activity against Israel, and negotiate agreement on an interim arrangement for a Palestinian Authority in Gaza and the West Bank, and to try to resolve all permanent status issues within five years.

I was sent as ambassador of the United States to meet with Arafat in Tunis in 1993. This was to be the first of many meetings. Arafat liked to play the host, insisting on serving our delegation lunch. We were about ten people around the table; four from the United States. A meal of roast chicken and potatoes had been prepared. Arafat was determined to not only serve the meal, but also to carve the chicken. Banter lightened the situation with words to the effect of, 'Are you actually going to cut my food for me as well?' with a reply of, 'If you like,' and my response of, 'No, thank you. The last person to cut my food was my mother.' Dessert followed and Arafat passed around an assortment of Arabic sweets such as *baklava* and *kanafi*, a Middle Eastern dessert made from cheese and brown sugar. The meal was, in fact, good and just what both parties needed to continue.

From then on food became part of the negotiation process. Denis fish is a variety of bream found in the Red Sea, so when I walked into a meeting, I would ask, 'Let me guess what we are eating today – Dennis fish?' Arafat would laugh, and at least in this context, he had a sense of humour. This repartee continued every time we met. I heard that even in my absence Arafat would mention this wordplay just to irritate the Israeli delegation.

~

When Shimon Peres was prime minister of Israel, he insisted that during negotiations the most important thing was to always find time to eat. So, suffice to say, there was always an abundance of food. Good food. Shimon knew I enjoyed eating salmon so an enormous amount would always be served. I remember joking with him, 'The Norwegians must be very happy; you are driving up the price of salmon just to satisfy me!'

Salmon Fillets with Green Peppercorn, Mushroom & Macadamia Nut Sauce

For salmon lovers

6 x 180g salmon fillets
garlic salt
2 lemons, juiced
15 macadamia nuts, roughly chopped
1 tablespoon flat-leaf parsley, finely
    chopped
1 tablespoon chives, finely chopped

SAUCE
50g butter
250g mushrooms, thinly sliced
1 lemon, juiced
1 tablespoon bottled green peppercorns,
    vinegar strained
1 garlic clove, crushed
salt and freshly ground pepper, to taste

Sprinkle the salmon fillets with garlic salt. Pour over lemon juice and marinate for 30 minutes. Grill or BBQ salmon, skin side down until almost cooked through. Turn and cook the other side for a minute or two.

Make sauce: Prepare whilst fish is cooking. Melt butter in a non-stick fry pan. Add mushrooms, lemon juice, peppercorns, garlic, salt and pepper and cook until mushrooms wilt and just begin to turn in colour.

Spoon sauce over fish and sprinkle with nuts and herbs.

(SERVES 6)

Ethan Zohn is a soccer player, charity worker, philanthropist, and winner of the 2001 television series, *Survivor: Africa*.

ETHAN ZOHN

He was born in 1973 in Lexington, Massachusetts, to Aaron and Rochelle. Ethan moved to New York and graduated in 1996 with a Bachelor of Arts in biology from Vassar College. After playing as a soccer goalkeeper at Vassar, he took up professional soccer.

Ethan was employed as a goalkeeper for the Highlanders Football Club in Zimbabwe, Cape Cod Crusaders in Massachusetts, and the Hawaii Tsunami in Oahu. He also played for the United States National Maccabiah Team in Israel in 1997 and 2001. He then coached the 2004 men's soccer team at the Pan American Maccabiah Games in Chile.

In 2002, using some of his *Survivor* prize-money, Ethan co-founded Grassroot Soccer, a non-profit organisation that trains Africa's professional soccer players to teach children about HIV/AIDS prevention. Since 2002, Grassroot Soccer has expanded to fifteen countries and graduated over 285,000 kids from the program. He is also a national spokesperson for America Scores, an organisation aimed at helping inner-city kids participate in educational soccer programs. His other charity work includes Autism Speaks, Colon Cancer Alliance, and Kick AIDS.

In recognition of his charity work, Ethan has received numerous awards including the 2004 Nkosi Johnson Community Spirit Award from the International Association of Physicians in AIDS Care, and Heroes Among Us Award from Boston Celtics and Massachusetts State Department.

Apart from his success in coaching, reporting and fundraising associated with soccer, Ethan has worked as a brand-name strategist and developer for new products. His many broadcast credits include a feature in the documentary film, *A Closer Walk*, along with the Dalai Lama, Bono and Kofi Annan; *Fear Factor*; and his own television show, *EarthTripping*, that focuses on eco-friendly travel and adventure.

Ethan is an aspiring inventor who enjoys scuba diving, photography, running and cooking. He currently lives in New York City.

Survival of the Fittest

My Jewish upbringing was a key factor in helping me win the reality television show, *Survivor: Africa*. I grew up knowing who I am, what I care about, and how I respond to challenges. Once you take away food and water, on top of being hungry and tired, one's true character and values come into focus.

I craved food leading up to, during and after *Survivor*; in fact, I became a little obsessed with food! For some crazy reason, pretty much the only thing I yearned for were buffalo wings (deep-fried chicken wings) and Rice Krispies treats. How bizarre: I'd been a vegetarian for fourteen years and yet when I arrived in Africa, the first thing I wanted was meat!

Over the course of 39 days the competitors had to find shelter, food and water while participating in physical and mental challenges. Those who succeeded were rewarded, often with food. I fast annually on *Yom Kippur* so I was already accustomed to hunger and this gruelling test of strength.

Food and religion came into 'flavouring' *Survivor*. During a reward challenge called 'Survivor Auction' each participant was given 20,000 Kenyan shillings. The contestants had to bid against each other to buy food items, the highest bidder being the winner. I won a jar of hot fudge. I teamed up with a guy named Big Tom. Together we won another mystery item to share: a full breakfast that was chock-full of pork – bacon, ham, cheese, eggs and pancakes. Big Tom had never met a Jewish person before which was pretty odd to me, and I'd never met anyone who had never met a Jewish person. I was now starving and hadn't eaten in 32 days. And here I was declining food. I explained that Jewish dietary laws prevented me from eating pork. I had never eaten these foods and they did not appeal to me. I just watched Big Tom devouring the bacon!

There were other challenges involving food. In 'Safari Supper', the teams were asked to feast like the tribes in East Africa had for thousands of years. A gross food challenge was to participate in an ancient Masai tradition of drinking cows' blood mixed with cows' milk … not so kosher! On winning another challenge, 'Get Your Goat', our tribe was rewarded with three egg-laying chickens and a rooster. Not only did I have to kill a chicken myself, I had to cook it and eat it! Yes, I ate it!

On my return I asked a rabbi if a starving person is allowed to break the dietary laws and eat *treif* (non-kosher food). The rabbi answered yes, it is permitted in times of survival. And I am indeed a *survivor!*

Blazing Hot Wing Sauce with Beer

A recipe from my friend John Schlimm, author of The Ultimate Beer Lover's Cookbook

SAUCE
1 packet Good Seasons Italian
   Dressing (powder)
½ cup margarine
2 cups Frank's Red Hot Cayenne
   Pepper Sauce
6 tablespoons beer

12–24 chicken wings or drumettes

Preheat oven to 180°C.

Make sauce: Combine all sauce ingredients in a bowl, mix well and set aside (makes 2¼ cups).

Make chicken wings: Boil wings in a large pot until they rise to the surface. Drain, place the wings into a baking dish and pour over sauce. Bake for 45 minutes or until crispy.

Note: This sauce can also be used as a dipping sauce for chicken tenders.

(SERVES 6)

Aussie-style Blazing Hot Wing Sauce with Beer

SAUCE
2 tablespoons McCormick Italian
   Seasoning Blend (dry)
½ cup margarine
1 cup white vinegar
1 cup water

2 teaspoons dried cayenne pepper
1 tablespoons hot pepper sauce
   (e.g. Tabasco)
6 tablespoons beer

12–24 chicken wings or drumettes

Preheat oven to 180°C.

Make sauce: Combine all ingredients in a bowl, mix well and set aside.

Make chicken wings: Prepare chicken wings as above.

(SERVES 6)

right: Professor Alan Crown with a Samaritan priest and a copy of one of their ancient Torah scrolls in the synagogue on Mt Gerizim at Kiryat Luza (1968).
below: Ethan Zohn working with children in Uganda for the organisation Grassroot Soccer, Inc.

below: Rabbi Shmuley with his family.

right: Phyllis Chesler with her mother, Lilian.

far top right: Dudu Fisher as a child.

above: Pnina Jacobson's family at a Rosh Hashanah dinner (left to right)
Rhona Adler (mother), Tilly Lax, Neville Gordon, Ray Gordon, Sam Adler (father).

Marinated Fresh Tuna Kebabs

2 large lemons
½ cup extra virgin olive oil
3 tablespoons light soy sauce
1kg tuna steaks, skin removed, cubed

8 bamboo skewers, soaked in water
¼ cup flat-leaf parsley, finely chopped
¼ cup chives, finely chopped (optional)

Place the zest and juice of 1 lemon in a shallow bowl. Add olive oil and soy sauce and whisk until well blended. Add tuna cubes and toss gently. Cover and marinate in the refrigerator for 2 hours.

Preheat a BBQ or grill plate, brush with oil and grill kebabs for 4–6 minutes, turning once; the tuna must be nicely browned, but still slightly rare in the middle. Cut extra lemon into wedges. Sprinkle tuna with parsley and chives and serve with lemon wedges.
(SERVES 4)

~

Salade Niçoise with Smoked Trout or Peppered Mackerel

200g green beans, top and tailed, cut in
    2cm pieces
½ iceberg or butter lettuce, torn into
    pieces
1 coral lettuce
1 punnet baby cherry tomatoes
2 Lebanese cucumbers, sliced
½ cup black olives, pitted
200g smoked trout or peppered
    mackerel, sliced into bite-sized pieces
4 eggs, hard-boiled and quartered
¼ red onion, thinly sliced (optional)
crusty bread, to serve

VINAIGRETTE
60ml olive oil
1 lemon, juiced
1 clove garlic, crushed
3 teaspoons Dijon mustard
freshly ground black pepper, to taste

Make vinaigrette: Place all ingredients in a screw-top jar and shake well.

Cook beans until just tender and bright green. Rinse under cold water. Arrange salad ingredients on a platter or on individual serving plates. Place trout and eggs on top and pour over vinaigrette. Serve immediately with a good crusty bread.
(SERVES 4)

Fresh Trout Fettuccine

1kg whole freshwater trout, cleaned,
    head and tail removed
500g fettuccine
olive oil
1 bunch fresh asparagus

125g snow peas
125g French green beans
rock salt flakes and black pepper, to taste
1 lemon, cut into wedges
grated Grana Padano or Romano cheese

Preheat oven to 180°C. Wrap the entire trout in foil and bake for about 30 minutes until the flesh comes away from the bones. Discard bones and skin and break the trout into chunks.

Cook pasta until just cooked (*al dente*). Drain.

Heat the oil in a wok or large frying pan. Stir-fry vegetables until cooked but still green.

Combine trout, vegetables and pasta and place in a large serving bowl. Season with rock salt and pepper. Serve with lemon wedges and cheese on the side.

(SERVES 4–6)

~

Exotic Chilli-Lime Fish Parcels

2 large banana leaves, each trimmed
    into 3 equal squares (3 x 30cm)
6 x 200g white fish fillets (such as
    snapper or flathead, rinsed and dried)
4 stalks lemongrass, trimmed and halved
2 spring onions, finely sliced, to garnish
2 red chillies, finely sliced, to garnish

CHILLI-LIME MARINADE
4 mild red chillies, seeded and
    finely sliced
2 gloves garlic, crushed
1 knob ginger (2–3cm), finely grated
1 tablespoon lime rind, finely grated
⅓ cup lime juice
1 cup coriander, chopped
1 cup light coconut cream

Preheat the oven to 220°C.

Make marinade: Combine all ingredients in a bowl and set aside.

Blanch each square of banana leaf in boiling water to prevent them from breaking when folding. Place each fish fillet into the centre of a banana leaf and top with a piece of lemongrass and some marinade. Turn in the sides and ends of the leaf to enclose the fish and secure with cocktail sticks or string. Spray with oil and bake for 10–15 minutes or until the fish is cooked through. Open parcels and garnish with spring onions and chillies.

Note: Aluminium foil can be used in place of banana leaves. Alternatively, parcels can be cooked under the grill or on the BBQ.

(SERVES 6)

BBQ Chicken with Zesty Sauce

1 extra large BBQ chicken, cut into 8 or
more pieces

2 tablespoons pine nuts

2 tablespoons unsalted roasted
cashew nuts

2 tablespoons preserved ginger,
very finely sliced

2 tablespoons flat-leaf parsley, chopped

1 tablespoon syrup from preserved ginger

3 tablespoons honey

2 teaspoons lemon zest

2 tablespoons vegetable oil

1 chicken stock cube, dissolved in ½ cup
boiling water

Preheat oven to 180°C. Place chicken in a large casserole dish.

Toast pine nuts in a frying pan over medium heat until golden and set aside.

Combine ginger, cashews, pine nuts and parsley and set aside.

Place ginger syrup, honey, lemon zest, oil and chicken stock in a small saucepan and heat until warm. Pour over chicken, turning so that each piece is well coated.

Cover and place in oven for about 30 minutes until heated through. Sprinkle nut mixture over the chicken. Serve with steamed rice.

(SERVES 4–6)

~

Barbecue Chicken Fillets with Chilli Mango Salsa

4 single chicken breasts, skin removed

¼ cup kecap manis (Indonesian sweet
soy sauce)

CHILLI MANGO SALSA

½ cup flat-leaf parsley, finely chopped

2 mangoes, cut into small cubes

1 red capsicum, seeded and cut into
small cubes

¼ red onion

1 tablespoon finely chopped mint
(optional)

½ cup sweet chilli sauce

Marinate chicken in kecap manis for 1 hour.

Make salsa: Gently combine all ingredients and refrigerate.

Heat a BBQ or chargrill plate, oil and cook chicken breasts for about 5 minutes on each side, until cooked through. Serve topped with salsa.

(SERVES 4)

Chicken Pearl *A favourite of Jeanne Pratt AO, an Australian philanthropist*

1 medium roasting chicken or 6
  drumsticks
½ cup plain flour, for dusting
salt and freshly ground black pepper
1 clove garlic, crushed
2 tablespoons oil
1 large onion, thinly sliced
1 green capsicum, diced

1 stalk celery, sliced
1 x 440g tin condensed tomato soup
  (such as Heinz)
5 capers in brine, drained and chopped
½ x 440g condensed tomato tin filled
  with water
pinch dried thyme or oregano

Cut chicken into 6–8 pieces. Combine flour, salt, pepper and garlic in a bowl and use to dust chicken pieces. Place in a dish, cover and refrigerate for 1 hour.

Heat oil in a frying pan. Fry chicken in batches until brown, remove from frying pan and set aside. Add onions, capsicum and celery to the same frying pan and fry until light brown. Pour off any excess oil.

Add tomato soup, water, capers and thyme or oregano to the frying pan and mix well. Return chicken to the frying pan, bring to the boil, reduce heat and simmer, covered, for about 1½ hours, until tender.

(SERVES 4–6)

~

Sweet Chilli & Balsamic Chicken

2 chickens, cut into pieces
1 cup firmly packed dark brown sugar
1 cup tomato sauce
¾ cup water
¼ cup oil (optional)

3 tablespoons balsamic vinegar
3 tablespoons soy sauce
1 small onion chopped
1 cup sweet chilli sauce

Preheat oven to 180°C. Place chicken into a greased roasting pan. Combine all other ingredients and pour over chicken. Bake, covered, for 1 hour. Uncover and cook until brown. Serve with rice or couscous.

(SERVES 6)

Osso Bucco

12 x 3–4cm thick pieces osso bucco
   (veal shanks)
4 tablespoons plain flour
2 teaspoons salt
½ teaspoon freshly ground black pepper
6 tablespoons olive oil

SAUCE
2 brown onions, finely diced
2 cloves garlic, crushed
2 medium carrots, finely diced
2 stalks celery, finely diced
1 x 400g tin crushed tomatoes
2 tablespoons tomato paste
1 cup beef stock, fresh or made using 1
   stock cube dissolved in 1 cup
   boiling water

1 cup dry white wine
1½ teaspoons dried oregano or few
   sprigs fresh oregano
1 teaspoon dried basil leaves or handful
   fresh basil
½ teaspoon dried thyme or few sprigs
   fresh thyme

GREMOLATA
3 tablespoons flat-leaf parsley, finely
   chopped
1 lemon, rind finely grated
1 clove garlic, crushed

Preheat oven to 180°C.

Dust veal shanks with flour, seasoned with salt and pepper. Heat oil in a large ovenproof dish and brown shanks on all sides, a few at a time. Set aside.

Make shanks: Dust veal shanks with flour, seasoned with salt and pepper. Heat oil in a large non-stick frying pan and brown shanks on all sides, a few at a time. Set aside.

Make sauce: Using the same frying pan, add onions, garlic, carrots and celery, stir well and cook until vegetables are soft. Add tomatoes, tomato paste, stock, wine and herbs and bring to the boil for a few minutes. Place the veal shanks into a large ovenproof dish and spoon over with the vegetable sauce. Cover and bake for about 1 hour stirring occasionally, until veal is tender. Add a little more stock or wine if necessary. Uncover and bake for a further 30 minutes.

Make gremolata: Combine parsley, lemon rind and garlic.

Sprinkle gremolata over the osso bucco before serving.

(SERVES 6)

G'Roestl Leftovers

2 tablespoons oil

2 tablespoon margarine

2 large onions, thinly sliced

4 cups cooked potatoes, sliced or cubed

4 cups cooked beef or chicken,
  thinly sliced

salt and freshly ground pepper, to taste

chopped flat-leaf parsley, for garnish

Heat half the oil and margarine in a large non-stick frying pan. Fry onions until golden, remove and set aside. Add remaining oil and margarine. Fry potatoes and when beginning to brown, add the meat. When crisp and brown, gently stir through onions. Add salt and pepper and serve, garnished with parsley.

(SERVES 4)

Bondi Steak Sandwich

1 tablespoon olive oil

4 large flat mushrooms

2 brown onions, finely sliced

4 beef one-minute steaks

8 slices sourdough bread, toasted

60g shredded lettuce or mixed baby
lettuce leaves

2 tomatoes, sliced

4 slices tinned beetroot, drained

tomato sauce or BBQ sauce

Heat oil in large non-stick frying pan over medium heat and gently sauté mushrooms until soft and set aside. Add onion to the pan and sauté until golden and set aside. Add steaks to the same pan and fry both sides over high heat.

Place 4 slices of bread on plates. Arrange lettuce, steak, tomatoes, beetroot and mushrooms on the bread. Top with a generous amount of sauce and the other slice of bread. Serve immediately.

(SERVES 4)

~

Gingered Thai Beef Salad

1kg sirloin beef steak

½ cup mint leaves, finely shredded

¼ cup lime juice

3 Lebanese cucumbers, seeded and
thinly sliced

1 cup bean shoots

½ red capsicum, sliced thinly into strips

125g baby cherry tomatoes, halved

mint leaves, for garnish

DRESSING

¼ cup coriander leaves or ½ tablespoon
dried coriander

2 cloves garlic, crushed

1 medium knob ginger, grated

2 tablespoons soy sauce

2 tablespoons lime juice

1 tablespoon white wine vinegar

1 tablespoon brown sugar

1 red chilli, finely sliced

Marinate beef in mint and lime juice and refrigerate for 3 hours.

Heat a frying pan or BBQ plate. Oil lightly and cook beef over high heat on all sides until medium rare. Allow to rest and cool.

Make dressing: Blend all ingredients in a food processor until smooth.

Using a very sharp knife, slice beef into thin strips and place in a bowl with cucumber, bean shoots, capsicums and tomatoes. Pour dressing over the salad and gently toss.

Garnish with extra mint leaves.

(SERVES 6)

Lettuce Delights

1 tablespoon sesame oil

1kg minced beef, chicken or veal

2 cloves garlic, crushed

1 teaspoon freshly grated ginger

1 small red capsicum, finely diced

1 stick celery, finely diced

1 can water chestnuts, sliced

¼ cup soy sauce

1 cup thick teriyaki sauce

½ x 50g packet fried noodles

6 iceberg lettuce leaves

GARNISH

thinly sliced spring onions

handful bean sprouts

extra fried noodles

Heat oil in a wok or large frying pan. Add mince, garlic and ginger and stir-fry until lightly browned. Add capsicum, celery, water chestnuts and sauces and stir-fry until vegetables are just tender. Remove from heat. On serving, gently stir through crispy noodles.

Fill lettuce leaves with the mixture and garnish.

(SERVES 6)

~

Waldorf Turkey Salad

1 cup Granny Smith apples, diced

1 lemon, juiced

4 cups turkey or chicken breasts, cooked
   and diced

4 celery sticks, thinly sliced

2 spring onions, finely sliced

¾ cup pecans or walnuts, chopped

½ cup red capsicum, finely diced

1 cup low-fat mayonnaise

1 tablespoons dill, finely chopped

salt and freshly ground black pepper,
   to taste

Combine lemon juice and apples in a large bowl, ensuring all pieces are coated well. Add turkey, celery, spring onions, nuts and capsicum. Gently stir through remaining ingredients and refrigerate until ready to serve.

(SERVES 4–6)

Veal in White Wine with Tarragon

8 veal escalopes, pounded thin
6 tablespoons plain flour, seasoned with
   salt and pepper
4 tablespoons margarine or oil
1 cup white wine
1 lemon, juiced
2 tablespoons tomato paste

1 teaspoon chopped fresh or 2
   teaspoons dried tarragon
1 teaspoon sweet paprika
1 x 425g tin whole baby champignon
   mushrooms, drained

Dust veal in flour. Melt margarine in a large non-stick frying pan and brown veal over high heat, in batches on both sides. Set aside.

Reduce heat. Using the same pan, add wine and mix well to scrape up all veal juices. Gently stir through remaining ingredients. Return veal to the pan and simmer for 10–15 minutes.

(SERVES 4)

Veal Piccante

2 tablespoons olive oil

8 veal escalopes, pounded thin

1 medium onion, thinly sliced

2 cloves garlic, crushed

⅓ cup water

1 teaspoon dried or 1 tablespoon fresh
    oregano

¼ cup dry white wine

salt and freshly ground black pepper,
    to taste

4 tablespoons tomato paste

1 x 400g tin chopped tomatoes in juice

½ cup black olives, pitted

1 tablespoon capers, drained

1 tablespoon flat-leaf parsley, finely
    chopped

Heat oil in a frying pan, add veal and brown, in batches. Set aside.

Using the same pan, fry the onions and garlic until soft. Add water and oregano and cook for a further minute. Add wine, salt, pepper, tomato paste and undrained tin tomatoes. Bring to the boil, reduce heat and simmer until sauce thickens.

Stir through olives and capers. Return veal to the pan to heat through in the sauce. Garnish with fresh parsley.

(SERVES 4)

~

Veal Tenderloins

1kg veal tenderloins

¼ cup light olive oil

1 sprig rosemary

GARNISH

¼ cup extra virgin olive oil

1 lemon, juiced

salt flakes and freshly ground black
    pepper, to taste

Marinate veal in light olive oil and rosemary for a few hours or overnight.

Preheat BBQ or grill. Grill veal for a few minutes, each side, so that all sides are cooked 1cm through and the centre is still pink. Leave to rest, covered, on a plate for 20 minutes.

Slice the veal on the diagonal and place on a serving dish. Drizzle with extra virgin olive oil and lemon juice, and sprinkle with salt and pepper.

(SERVES 4)

Something Sweet

- Apple Petrover: Apple Bread & Butter Pudding
- Mini Espresso Cupcakes
- Rich Chocolate Truffles
- Csusztatott Palacsinta: Slip Pancake
- Elegant Chocolate Mousse Gâteaux
- Coffee Meringue Ice Cream
- Fête Fare: Mini Cheeseless Cheese Cakes
- Lemon Angel Cake
- Morello Cherry Strudel
- Buchti: 'Little Pillows'
- French Apple Tarte; Fresh Apple Kuchen
- Honey Glace Slice
- Toblerone Chocolate Mousse
- Marlee's Secret Oatmeal Chocolate Chip Cookies
- Choc Prune Pecan Log
- My Grandmother Mitzi's Chocolate Cake
- New York Egg-Cream
- Celebration Fruit Slice
- Viola's Marzipan and Strawberry Diamonds
- Rosé Jelly with Mixed Berries; Date & Ginger Balls
- Fruit Galette; Ginger Snaps
- Nana's Custard Biscuits
- Rocky Road; Mini Florentines

RABBI RAYMOND APPLE

Rabbi Raymond Apple AO RFD, historian and writer, is emeritus rabbi of the Great Synagogue, Sydney.

Born and educated in Melbourne, Australia, he pursued rabbinic studies in England at Jews' College, now called the London School of Jewish Studies. He has degrees from various universities and is an honorary fellow of Sydney University and a Doctor of Laws (*honoris causa*) from the University of NSW.

He was senior rabbi of the Great Synagogue for 32 years after holding pulpits at two London congregations. He has been active in interfaith and community affairs for many years and was Australia's highest-profile rabbi. He was a judge of the Sydney Beth Din (the ecclesiastical court) and senior rabbi to the Australian Defence Force as well as holding office in many other organisations. He is an eminent Freemason and has written on Masonic as well as Jewish and Australian history, and has published several books.

Rabbi Apple and his wife Marian have four adult children and a number of grandchildren. They now live in Israel but visit and lecture in Australia from time to time.

'Ess Kindelach, Ess!' ('Eat Children, Eat!')

Our ancestors in the wilderness wanted fish, cucumbers, melons, leeks and garlic – and all they got was manna. No matter that the manna was regular, reliable and versatile in taste. No matter that this was the desert and it was a miracle that there was any food at all. They needed something to complain about and the food was the first thing that came to mind. Maybe this was the beginning of the age-old Jewish obsession with food?

The apocryphal Jewish mother thinks that food (especially chicken soup) is the cure of all ills. *'Ess kindelach, ess!'* is her way of handling every problem. If anyone is not hungry she takes it as a personal insult ('What's wrong with you that you're not eating?' she demands; 'You don't love me – it was me who made the food!'). It's a joke, but every joke has its serious side. If you eat well you feel well. If you feel well you think well. If you think well you can face what life brings. If you can face what life brings you can find a way through. It all begins with food.

That's part of the reason I often find myself in the kitchen. It's not in spite of being a rabbi but because of it. I want people to be able to handle life, and if I can help by contributing to what they eat, I'm pleased. But I need the kitchen for other reasons too. When the rabbinic responsibility gets on top of me – and it's a calling with more than its share of aggravation and pressure – cooking is a form of therapy. Not that I'm a chef or even a particularly good cook, but I can cope with most things – though in our family we make it difficult by not only being kosher but by having a non-meat home.

So what do I cook? I enjoy creating vegetarian dishes, though it's all generally *ad hoc*. I don't use recipe books. Nor do I always remember exactly what went into a particular dish so things don't necessarily taste the same the second time round. My wife will say, 'What have you made?' One answer is, 'A mess' – though I do try to clean up after myself. The better answer is, 'A *petrover*' – one of those phrases you can't completely translate into good English. My *petrovers* often use up leftovers, especially leftover *challah*.[1] I can make a *challah petrover* savoury or I can make it sweet.

---

1   *challah* – traditional braided bread.

If you eat well you feel well. If you feel well you think well. If you think well you can face what life brings. If you can face what life brings you can find a way through. It all begins with food.

above: Rabbi Apple at the Great Synagogue, Sydney (2002).
below: With Australian artist, Robert Hannaford.

Rabbi Apple's 'Petrover'

Petrover

Leftover *challah* (how much? – it depends on what you didn't eat on *Shabbat*)

Fruit juice (apple is best – what else when Apple is my surname?)

Oil (instinct will tell you how much)

1 egg (or 2 if you want)

Honey or golden syrup (personally I don't use sugar, but you might decide to)

Sultanas (a generous handful)

Spices – cinnamon, ginger (enough to give a taste)

Ground almonds or other nuts (you work out how much)

Dried fruit (or fresh – you decide!)

Knead the *challah* in fruit juice.

Mix well with egg/s, oil, honey (or golden syrup).

Mix in the other ingredients.

Put the lot in a greased baking dish (preferably *pareve*[2] but with us it doesn't matter because we have no *fleishig*[3]).

Bake until the aroma fills the house and you think it's ready.

2   *pareve* – any food containing neither meat nor milk derivatives and may be used at either meat or milk meals.
3   *fleishig* – any food containing meat, fowl or their derivatives.

Apple Petrover: Apple Bread & Butter Pudding

A delicious interpretation of Rabbi's recipe

PETROVER

4 medium Granny Smith apples

40g unsalted butter

1 large brioche or 1 medium *challah* bread, sliced evenly and buttered

1 lemon, juiced

4 tablespoons sultanas (optional – soaked in brandy or calvados)

½ cup walnuts or pecans, roughly chopped

1 tablespoon brown sugar

2 tablespoons Demerara sugar

extra butter for greasing

icing sugar for dusting

double cream or vanilla ice-cream to serve

CUSTARD

4 large eggs

300ml single cream

400ml milk

2½ tablespoons caster sugar

1 teaspoon ground cinnamon

½ teaspoon ground ginger

Preheat the oven to 180°C.

Make the custard: Whisk all ingredients in a bowl and set aside.

Make the pudding: Peel, core and slice apples. Pour lemon juice over to avoid browning. Grease a 2-litre ovenproof dish and line with half the buttered bread. Layer the apple slices on top and sprinkle with sultanas, nuts and brown sugar. Pour half the custard over the apples. Evenly layer remaining bread over the top and pour remaining custard over the bread. Leave to absorb for about 5 minutes. Sprinkle Demerara sugar over pudding. Bake for 45 minutes to 1 hour on middle shelf. Remove when golden and custard has set.

Serve warm, dusted with icing sugar. Place a dollop of cream or vanilla ice-cream on the side.

(SERVES 8–10)

IAN BERSTEN

Ian Bersten is an expert on coffee and an author. He was born in 1939 in Sydney, Australia.

His father Mischa was born in Kiev, Ukraine. His mother Adele Charlotte De Groen was born in Sydney, the granddaughter of a Dutch immigrant from Rotterdam who came to Australia in 1859. The first immigrant in her family was a convict, Mordechai Moses, who arrived in 1836 and later became the *shammas* or guardian of the York Street Synagogue.

In 1968, Ian established Belaroma, a coffee-roasting factory and coffee shop in Sydney. His passion for coffee led him to amass one of the largest collections of coffee antiques in the world together with a significant library of books dating from 1682. Ian has written a number of books including *Coffee Floats Tea Sinks: A History of Coffee and Coffee Technology* and *Coffee, Sex and Health: History of Anti-Coffee Crusaders and Sexual Hysteria* that traces the history of bizarre medical and sexual theories relating to tea and coffee.

After graduating with a commerce degree from the University of NSW, Ian worked for more than 36 years in the coffee business, travelling overseas to buy coffee and presiding over judging and tasting panels. He set up a specialist shop, The Coffee Bean Genie, in Roseville to sell coffee and equipment. Ian is now involved in the creation of Tea-Cha, a tea cappuccino process.

Ian lives in Sydney with his wife Helen, an archivist who was awarded an OAM for her services to the Australian Jewish community. They have three daughters.

An Expert on Coffee

I'm an old hand in the coffee industry which tries to tell people that the quality of the coffee in the cup depends on whether it was picked by a twelve-year-old virgin at 7.30 am while the sun rises in the east and the dew is still on the leaves.

My interest in coffee may have begun when I was a child. I can still see myself standing on a chair watching a saucepan of milk and water being heated on the stove to make coffee and it being removed just before it started to boil over.

I can still remember the two best cups of coffee I've ever had. I'm sure if I had them today they probably wouldn't rate at all because I believe that when you taste something for the first time, it's never as good again. When you eat European white asparagus in Luxembourg or special Italian chocolate that leaves your tongue *frizzante* or salmon smoked in hickory chips in Seattle – they are the best tastes.

So let me tell you about the first best cup of coffee I ever had. I was in Utrecht on my way to the Douwe Egbert coffee factory to learn about coffee. I was staying in a little hotel, nothing special, probably two stars. A cup of coffee was given to me and my taste-buds lit up – wow! – what had they done? It was filter coffee, a product I'd been selling in Sydney for years.

I spoke to one of the experts at the Douwe Egbert factory. It all became clear. In Australia we used 70 grams per jug in a filter machine and in Holland they used 110 grams – over fifty percent more. Then came a discussion of the machine. The Australian machine brewed coffee at who knows what temperature; I suspect it was around 80°C. The Dutch machine brewed at 92°C and the extract was terrific. I later learnt that the machine had been invented by a Willy Brandl from Zurich who came up with the first electric filter coffee machine in 1944. I have never had another cup of filter coffee as good.

The next best cup of coffee I had was an espresso in Nice, France. I had taken a sample of my own brand of coffee and was introduced to the chief tasting and brewing technician at one of Europe's best coffee-machine manufacturers. The company had been started by the grandfather, an Italian engineer, Mario Levi, in 1918 and they were very strong on engineering. Norbert, the Portuguese brewing expert, tasted my coffee and was impressed. He asked me to wait while he set up the machine for my coffee. He changed the grinds, the brewing temperature of the machine, the heat exchanger and tried a taste at every change. Finally he asked me to taste the coffee. The flavour exploded in my mouth; never before and never since has an espresso coffee tasted as good.

At least I am able to say I have had two really outstanding cups of coffee in my life among a lot of just plain good ones. Here's to great coffee.

Mini Espresso Cupcakes
Ecco un vero caffè dolci!

2 eggs
¾ cup caster sugar
½ cup milk
1 teaspoon vanilla essence
1 cup plain flour
½ cup ground hazelnuts
2 teaspoons baking powder
¼ teaspoon salt
125g unsalted butter, melted
mini cupcake paper cases

decoration – coffee beans or chocolate-coated coffee beans

ESPRESSO BUTTER CREAM ICING
100g unsalted butter, softened
150g icing sugar, or extra if needed
2 teaspoons espresso coffee or 2 teaspoons instant coffee dissolved in 1 teaspoon water

Preheat oven to 180°C. Place mini cupcake cases onto a tray.
Make cupcakes: Beat eggs and sugar until light and fluffy. Slowly pour in milk and vanilla. Stir in flour, hazelnuts, baking powder and salt. Add butter and beat until well mixed. Spoon batter into paper cases until ¾ full and smooth top with metal spatula. Bake for about 10 minutes, until golden. Allow to cool completely before icing.

   Make icing: Cream icing sugar and butter together until fluffy. Add extra icing sugar if not quite stiff, then slowly add coffee until icing becomes fluffy and spreadable.

   Pipe or spread espresso icing over the cupcakes and decorate each one with a chocolate-coated coffee bean.
(MAKES 24 MINI OR 12 MEDIUM-SIZED CUPCAKES)

MAX BRENNER

Max Brenner is a chocolatier and businessman. He was born in Haifa, Israel, in 1968, the son of Gideon and Tova.

In 1996, Max Brenner – Chocolate by the Bald Man was established as a partnership between Max Fichtman and Oded Brenner in Ra'anana with the aim of designing a new chocolate culture. Chocolate accessories such as cups and hug mugs, packaging, and all forms of presentations were created. The philosophy was: 'Chocolate portrays romance, sensuality, passion, addiction, prestige, warmth, sex, love and nostalgia.'

In 2001 Strauss-Elite bought the Max Brenner brand-name, operating the financial and manufacturing business with Max maintaining his management and creative role. Today, Max Brenner has stores worldwide including in Israel, Australia, the UK and the US and distributes products to prestigious hotels and gourmet stores around the world.

Max currently lives in New York.

Sailing Down a River of Chocolate

All I really ever wanted to do was write. I started, I had the passion, but I haven't published anything yet. I loved everything that was associated with writing – beautiful pens and paper and, above all, the notion of finding my small corner where I could create. My other passion was reading. When I was ten years old, inspired by *Charlie and the Chocolate Factory*, I dreamt that I would sail down a river of chocolate.

After finishing my compulsory Israeli army service, I was ready to write. But I needed money to support myself. I heard about government-funded trade apprenticeships and chose to become a pastry chef because it seemed the easiest and the cleanest of professions offered. My parents Tova and Gideon were not happy with my decision. My father, like so many, was liberal-minded until it came to his own children. 'You should go to university to study mathematics, law ... all your friends from high school are going to be accountants and lawyers and you are going to be left behind. And you will regret it.' I simply said, 'No, I don't think so.'

I went to work in Europe, learning from many pastry masters. I intended to write after finishing each job, but it just never happened. I kept finding excuses and postponing my big dream. In a small business in Paris, I learnt to make delicate handmade chocolates, marzipan and toffees. There I listened to stories, learning things that can only be passed on by word of mouth. With payment only in work experience, I ran out of money and had to go back to Israel.

Back home, employed as a consultant in a chain of coffee shops, I met a young religious new immigrant from Denmark. His name was Max Fichtman, a baker, and he was planning to open a bakery. Together we decided to start a different business. He was the entrepreneur with the finance and I brought the knowledge. We opened our first chocolate store in Ra'anana, with a tiny shopfront and kitchen behind. We were both just 26.

Chocolate flows in my veins. My grandparents on my father's side came to Israel from Prague in 1939. My grandfather went to Egypt after joining the British army and my grandmother needed to work. She set up a small kitchen making handmade pralines dipped in chocolate with Brandl, a chocolatier from Prague, selling them door-to-door to the European immigrants who craved these delicacies and a link to their culture back home. Sadly, she never mentioned this to me and never lived to see the opening of my first store.

Universally, children love chocolate. I would look forward to every Friday night when my grandparents would bring a chocolate treat. It would be the same tablet

My grandfather went to Egypt after joining the British army and my grandmother needed to work. She set up a small kitchen making handmade pralines dipped in chocolate with Brandl, a chocolatier from Prague, selling them door-to-door to the European immigrants who craved these delicacies and a link to their culture back home.

above: Max Brenner with his grandmother.
below: Max Brenner with his mother, Tova.

of Elite milk chocolate with its red paper wrapper decorated with the cow logo, which had money slipped inside.

Every year, my parents went skiing without us children. Being little, I would run to greet them in my pyjamas on their return and excitedly watch them open their suitcases filled with chocolates, mostly from Austria. Each of us three children received thirty tablets (blocks). I can still describe each package and even now, some twenty years later, these brands are still on supermarket shelves. The little Austrian chocolate wafer, Manner, was so precious then but today it's everywhere in every kiosk. I don't buy it myself but wait to receive it as a gift to remember and savour its uniqueness.

We had a family ritual that contributes to my love of chocolate. As a child, the only chocolate available was a 200 gram bar and it looked enormous to me. Our weekly ceremony would begin after lunch on Fridays. My father would slowly and deliberately take out the bar and count the cubes, as if he didn't know how many there were. He took a knife and with precision, cut the slab into 32 cubes – ten, ten, ten and one each for my mother and himself. You could hear him cutting the original chocolate paper wrapper into pieces and carefully re-wrapping the portions. My brother Dror and I ate ours immediately but my sister Iris would not finish hers. Over the next few days I would try to bribe her for pieces.

Chocolate has filled my life. My dream of sailing down a river of chocolate lives on from the success of the Max Brenner stores. John Lennon said, 'Life is what happens while you are busy making other plans.' And I will write my novel...

My dream of sailing down a river of chocolate lives on from the success of the Max Brenner stores.

Rich Chocolate Truffles
Favourites from the Bald Man

DARK RASPBERRY TRUFFLES

BASIC RECIPE

400g dark chocolate caibos (choc chips) or blocks broken into small pieces

200ml double cream (45–53% fat content)

50g unsalted butter, cut into cubes

80ml raspberry liqueur

80g fine cocoa powder

Place butter and cream in a saucepan over medium heat. When the butter starts to melt, stir in chocolate. Add raspberry liqueur and continue stirring until the mixture is smooth and shiny. Pour truffle mixture into airtight container and refrigerate overnight. Wearing disposable gloves, roll teaspoons of the truffle mixture into balls and roll in fine cocoa powder.

(MAKES 30–35 PIECES)

MILK HAZELNUT TRUFFLES

Follow basic recipe, substituting the dark chocolate with milk chocolate and omitting the raspberry liqueur. Roll truffle balls in 80g coarsely chopped roasted hazelnuts and coat well.

WHITE CHILLI TRUFFLES

Follow basic recipe, substituting the milk chocolate with white chocolate and the raspberry liqueur for ¼ teaspoon of cayenne pepper after the chocolate has melted. Mix well. Roll truffle balls in desiccated coconut instead of fine cocoa powder.

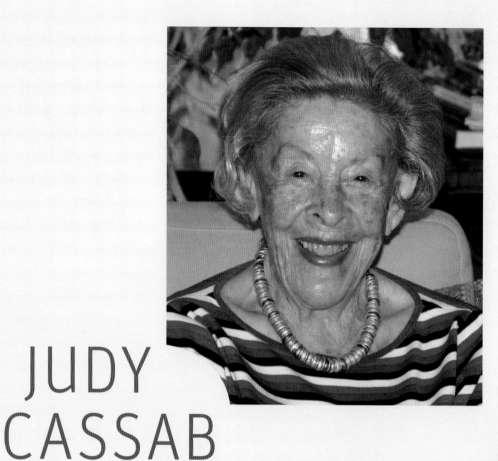

JUDY CASSAB

Judy Cassab (Kaszab) CBE AO is a renowned artist.

She was born in Vienna, Austria, in 1920, the daughter of Imre and Ilona.

Shortly after marrying, the Nazis sent Judy's husband Jancsi to a forced labour camp. He was freed in 1944 and the couple moved to Hungary. In late 1950, the Australian government granted Judy and her family permission to settle in Australia as displaced persons. Judy initially worked as an art teacher and spent her weekly earnings on a housekeeper so she could develop her own painting style.

On winning the five-hundred-guinea Women's Weekly Prize in 1955 and 1956, Judy's talent as a portrait artist was recognised. This prize-money funded a trip to Europe where she was finally able to fulfil her dream of studying the great masters. Judy is best known as a portrait painter. Her subjects include socialites, aristocracy and royalty from all over the world.

Judy has won more than thirteen major awards, including Australia's prestigious Archibald Prize in 1961 and 1968. She has been awarded the Order of Australia and made Companion to the Order of the British Empire in recognition of her contribution to the arts. In 1995, she was awarded a Doctor of Letters (*honoris causa*) from Sydney University. Judy's works are displayed in the National Gallery of Australia, in state galleries, and in public and private collections throughout the world. She has also published books and continues to give of her time to her family and community.

Judy lives in Sydney, Australia.

'I'm Going to Be Another Michelangelo.'

My parents divorced when I was twelve, my mother taking me to live with my grandmother in Beregslasz, a small town in Hungary which became Czechoslovakia. I grew up with two uncles, an aunt, my mother and grandmother, and in this large loving family, I had a very happy childhood.

When I was twelve years old I started painting and writing a diary. There was no gallery or art school, but this did not dim my enthusiasm. I kept painting as if I was going to be another Master. If my mother had consulted an expert about my ability, the answer would have been, 'Not a hope!' But in my heart, I would have thought: 'You fool, you don't know I'm going to be another Michelangelo.'

I matriculated from school and joined a debating team. A gentleman by the name of Jancsi Kampfner, a director of a brewery in Podhering, sat in the audience with my friend Feri. Jancsi proposed just three weeks later and although he was twice my age, he assured me that this age difference would matter less as time went by.

But before getting married I had to follow my dream and he sent me off for a year to the Academy of Art in Prague to study painting, saying, 'This is so you don't think in five years: "Oh, if only I could have studied then!"' With this wise decision he completely charmed me and I was quite sick with love!

In 1938, the Germans came. We heard a tremendous roar in the streets and looking out of the windows we saw their tanks thundering in to occupy Prague. My studies were cut short and I knew I had to get home. I had to get my travel papers from the German embassy. I kept hearing the shout, 'Jews to the end of the queue!'. For the first time in my life I was not a human being, only a Jew.

After three days my papers were stamped and I left. Jancsi and I married in 1939. Shortly after, Jancsi was sent to forced labour camps in Poland and Kiev and I was alone between 1941 and 1944. Corresponding by letter was not allowed, so before he left, we chose a certain star in the sky to look upon and meet there every night. Jancsi later told me that this connection saved his life. In 1949, after suffering ten years of oppression in Hungary and using our Czech passports, Jancsi and I moved with our two young boys to Vienna.

The hard times make you remember the good times. The shelves in my grandmother's pantry overflowed with colourful glass jars filled with different types of preserved foods. These were my grandmother's pride and joy. There was no such thing as canned food. I remember picking the yellow and red cherries from our cherry orchard and little wild strawberries from the countryside. Conserving

top left: Judy, aged fourteen, with her mother Ilona and aunt Ami.

top right: Judy outside an art gallery in London where she had a one-person exhibition (1981).

above: Judy's father, Imre Kaszab.

above right: Judy and Jancsi at the Devil's Marbles, Northern Territory, Australia.

right: Judy with Jansci, Johnny and Peter (1955);

fruit from our garden was a festive occasion and everyone helped with the preparations. The smell was delicious as the fruit boiled with the sugar. Carefully, the fruit would be placed in clean glass jars and stored, later to be used in my grandmother's wonderful cooking. I can still taste her cherry slip-pancakes.

I clearly remember we ate one goose a week because the fat (lard) was collected in large containers for the winter. Every edible part of this goose would be used. Having goose liver and crackling for lunch was the norm. We would take the breast meat off the bone, put it through the mincer and make a meatloaf with garlic and chopped onions. This mixture was moulded back on top of the bone and baked. A real feat of sculpture!

The recipes I use today date back to those years. I recall words of praise from our dear friend Desiderius Orban, the great artist and teacher, when he came to dinner, 'Oh, why does such a woman paint?'

The hard times make you remember the good times. The shelves in my grandmother's pantry overflowed with colourful glass jars filled with different types of preserved foods.

Csusztatott Palacsinta: Slip Pancake

A sweet success

VANILLA SUGAR
½ vanilla bean
1 cup icing sugar or caster sugar

5 eggs, separated
50g unsalted butter, softened
50g caster sugar
50g plain flour
1 cup milk
extra butter or oil spray, for frying

Make vanilla sugar: Break vanilla pod into pieces, crush in a blender, stir through the sugar and set aside.

Make slip pancake: Beat egg whites until stiff. In a separate bowl, cream butter and sugar until light and fluffy, beat in egg yolks and add in flour and milk. Gently fold in egg whites. Heat a 20cm crepe pan until moderately hot and melt butter or spray with oil. Place a large soup ladle of pancake mixture into the pan and fry it **only** on one side. When set, slip it onto a 20cm ovenproof round plate. Sprinkle some vanilla sugar on top. Make the next pancake. Stack this over the first one and repeat the process until five thick pancakes have been cooked. Cut into slices like a torte. This can be served at once or prepared ahead of time and reheated for about 15 minutes in a hot oven.

Note: Savoury alternative: To make as an entrée, sprinkle each slip pancake layer with grated cheese and finely sliced mushrooms.
(SERVES 8–10)

Europe... a feast for the eyes!

Naomi Chazan is a world-renowned professor of political science, a peace activist, author, and a former member of the Israeli Knesset, Israel's legislative body.

NAOMI CHAZAN

Naomi was born in 1946 in Jerusalem to Abe and Zena Harman, English Zionists who immigrated to Israel in 1940.

She served for eleven years in the Knesset. In 1992 she was elected as a member of the newly formed Meretz party and retained her seat until 2003. She served as deputy speaker of the Knesset from 1996 to 2003 and has also been a member of many legislative committees.

Throughout her career, Naomi has worked for the advancement of the status of women in Israel and for peace between Israelis and Palestinians. Naomi has degrees in political science and African studies from the Hebrew University in Jerusalem. She co-founded the Israel Women's Network, the Israel Women's Peace Net, Bat Shalom, Engendering the Peace Process, and the International Commission for Just and Sustainable Israeli–Palestinian Peace.

She was a member of Israel's delegation to the United Nations Conference on Women in Nairobi in 1985 and Beijing in 1995. Naomi was president of the Israeli branch of the Society for International Development, vice-president of the International Association of Political Science, and headed the Truman Research Institute for the Advancement of Peace at the Hebrew University of Jerusalem.

She has published books and papers on comparative politics, women's rights and Israel–Arab relations. She is the recipient of numerous awards including the Freedom and Human Rights Prize from the Foundation for Freedom and Human Rights in Switzerland, and Twentieth Anniversary Honoree for Lifetime Contribution to the Advancement of Women from Israel Women's Network. She speaks Hebrew, English, French, and some Swahili.

Naomi lives in Jerusalem and has two children.

Belgian Chocolate Breaks Down Barriers

I was told that from the moment I was born I was nourished on chocolate milk instead of fresh milk. Perhaps this explains my love of chocolate. Over time it became my prime comfort food, giving me a sense of contentment and wellbeing. I'm sure this is true for so many people; after all, the Aztecs called chocolate the elixir of the gods.

In May 1989 in Brussels, Israeli and Palestinian women gathered for the first time for a serious discussion. We were about forty women who represented public opinion from both sides. Among us were Shulamit Aloni, Hanan Ashrawi, Leila Shahid, Yael Dayan and Zaheera Kamal. Initially, needless to say, there was a tremendous amount of suspicion. The atmosphere was strained and we had great difficulty communicating with each other. I was getting very worried about what was happening; there seemed to be no way of crossing the bridge, of transcending the emotional baggage each of us carried at the height of the first intifada (Palestinian uprising against Israeli rule in the West Bank and Gaza Strip from 1987 to 1993). When this first difficult session was over, I thought I would take advantage of being in Brussels.

What a wonderful opportunity to go on a chocolate-buying spree! Brussels is the chocolate capital of the world. I wandered into many different chocolate ateliers and shops – and there are a lot in Brussels, over 2000! I bought a variety from the specialty chocolate artisans and houses, including the better-known ones, such as Godiva's, Leonidas and Neuhaus, as well as from smaller shops that produce simply superb creations. Pierre Marcolini is one of my favourites. These beautiful chocolates are made from scratch using the world's best ingredients – cacao beans from Venezuela, butter from France, vanilla from Madagascar and almonds from Portugal.

That evening, I invited the delegates to a chocolate-tasting party. It was an impromptu gathering that started with three or four women and slowly grew to almost twenty. I said that Brussels is the place where, no matter what you thought about each other, you might as well enjoy the food. Using airline sleeping masks to cover our eyes, we spent hours sampling these delicacies, trying to figure out which were the best chocolates. What a problem!

Perhaps this is what politicians need to make constructive beginnings? The outcome of the conference was very positive. It led to the promise of further dialogue between our women and to over twenty years of ongoing cooperation. So my advice is, if you have problems, try eating chocolates with somebody. It may help.

Elegant Chocolate Mousse Gâteaux

Real chocolate lovers can eat the mousse alone

1 chocolate pound cake or chocolate
   sponge
4 teaspoons liqueur, such as Sabra or
   Tia Maria
1 quantity chocolate mousse
150g white chocolate
300ml fresh cream, whipped stiffly
icing sugar to decorate
raspberries, fresh or defrosted frozen,
   to decorate

CHOCOLATE MOUSSE
200g dark bittersweet chocolate (good
   quality)
1 tablespoon butter/margarine
4 eggs, separated
1 teaspoon vanilla essence
2 tablespoons caster sugar

Make cake base: Line base of 4 x 100ml ramekins with a circle of baking paper. Slice cake
into 10mm thick pieces and cut out 4 rounds, the size of the top of the ramekin, and
drizzle each with 1 teaspoon of liqueur. Set aside.

Make mousse: Using a double boiler, melt chocolate and butter. Lightly beat egg yolks
and vanilla with a fork and stir into chocolate mixture. Beat egg whites until very stiff,
slowly adding the sugar. Fold chocolate mixture **into** egg whites. Spoon equal quantities
of mousse into prepared ramekins. Place each cake base on top of mousse and gently
press down. Cover ramekins with cling wrap and allow to set in the refrigerator for at
least 2 hours.

Make chocolate shard decoration: Line a tray with baking paper. Using a double boiler,
melt white chocolate. Spread melted chocolate evenly over the paper. Cover chocolate
with another piece of baking paper and gently roll to form a thin sheet of chocolate. Place
in the refrigerator until set and break into 100mm length pieces.

To serve: Run a hot knife around inside edge of each ramekin to loosen the gâteau.
Place a plate over the top, turn out and remove the paper circle. Dust each serving plate
with icing sugar and place a mousse in the centre. Cover the top with whipped cream and
decorate generously with raspberries. Decorate with two white shards, dust again with a
little icing sugar and place a few raspberries on the side.

(SERVES 4)

SHARON GLASS

Sharon Glass is a chef and author.

Born in Johannesburg, South Africa, she had no formal training as a cook but as a young child was inspired by her mother. The family immigrated to California in 1977.

While studying at UCLA, Sharon began working part-time for celebrity Danny Kaye. He was also an avid cook and a major influence on her life, teaching her many interesting tips and recipes and allowing her to help prepare some wonderful meals for his friends and famous chefs. After graduating, Sharon continued working as his personal assistant and with her mother also managed a catering business.

Sharon returned to South Africa in 1984 with her husband Anthony and began a small catering business and cookery school. She juggled her growing career as a caterer and teacher with being a mother of three children.

Sharon's highly successful first cookbook, *Simply Delicious*, was published in 2000. This was followed by *Simply Too Delicious* and *Absolutely Delicious*. She has travelled all over the world giving cooking demonstrations and promoting her cookbooks.

No Such Thing as a Disaster in the Kitchen

I have always been at home in the kitchen. I grew up helping my mother, cooking and creating. As I spent more and more time in the kitchen, it was a natural progression to pursue a profession in food preparation, teaching and demonstrating this art that I find so rewarding. Demonstrations usually work perfectly but occasionally things can go horribly wrong. These are the ones you tend to remember.

Cape Town is one of the most beautiful cities in South Africa. It was here that I'd rented a demonstration kitchen with a spectacular view. During my demonstrations I usually show how to prepare a dish and have a finished product on display as well. On one particular day, my signature dish was a meringue. When I opened the foil that was covering the perfect meringue I'd made two days earlier, the damp coastal air of Cape Town had turned it into a pancake. I nearly died! What to do? I had to pretend in front of 75 people that there was no problem – not an easy task. Experience has taught me not to show any signs of anguish and to simply smile and continue.

I decided there and then to make an ice-cream meringue Swiss roll. All I had to do was make some ice-cream, spread it onto the flat meringue and roll it up. After freezing the concoction, I liberally dusted it with icing sugar and sliced it. *Voilà*, a perfect mistake! An absolute stunner! No one could believe the dessert was actually a flop. My moral of this story is never tell about a disaster in the kitchen but rather pretend that you have just created a new dish.

~

At Pick 'N Pay, a busy supermarket chain in South Africa, I enlisted a good friend to assist me in a demonstration. I was preparing a whole poached fish with a tomato sauce. I had already spilled some liquid on the floor and my friend was inconspicuously crouching below, wiping up the mess under my feet, ensuring I would not slip. At the same time I was trying to balance a very large tray of fish. The tray misbalanced, and with that some of the hot tomato sauce spilled down my friend's back, causing her to laugh uncontrollably! She refused to get up from the floor in front of eighty people and tried to crawl to the scullery behind me. The managing director's wife happened to be in the audience and went to the clothing division to find a fresh T-shirt for her to wear. To this day, during every fish demonstration I am reminded of my giggling friend covered in a smelly hot red tomato sauce.

Coffee Meringue Ice-Cream

A sweet indulgence

MERINGUE
4 egg whites
2 tablespoons instant coffee powder
1 cup caster sugar
ice-cream
100g dark chocolate
100g white chocolate

COFFEE ICE-CREAM
4 eggs, separated
¾ cup caster sugar
2½ tablespoons instant coffee powder
1 teaspoon vanilla essence
1 cup cream (or non-dairy alternative)
1 x 80g box vanilla instant pudding (or equivalent)

Make ice-cream: Beat egg yolks, sugar, coffee and vanilla essence until thick. In a separate bowl, beat egg whites until very stiff. In another bowl, beat cream until very thick and mix in the vanilla instant pudding. Fold all three mixtures together and freeze until set.

Make meringue: Preheat oven to 120°C. Line a baking tray with baking paper and spray with oil. Beat egg whites with coffee powder until very stiff. Add sugar, a little at a time, and beat very well for about 20 minutes until egg whites resemble marshmallows. Spoon meringue onto baking tray and mould to form a round basket with a low wall. Bake for 1 hour. Turn off oven and allow meringue to cool in oven before removing.

Make chocolate decoration: Melt dark and white chocolate separately in different bowls over simmering water. Pour or spoon melted chocolates in dollops over one large piece of baking paper. Using a skewer, drag the various sections of chocolate together to create a marbled effect. Immediately cover with another piece of baking paper and roll out with a rolling pin. When the chocolate is uniformly thin, allow to harden in refrigerator. Crack hardened chocolate into shards.

To serve: Allow ice-cream to soften slightly before spooning onto meringue. Decorate with chocolate pieces.

(SERVES 8–10)

HIRSH GOODMAN

250

Hirsh Goodman is a journalist, author and senior research associate at the Jaffee Center for Strategic Studies at Tel Aviv University.

He was born in 1946 in Port Elizabeth, South Africa, the son of Ginda and Leib. Like most South African Jews, his parents escaped the pogroms in Latvia (or Lithuania, depending on the position of the border at any given time).

Having grown up white and Jewish in apartheid South Africa, Hirsh, filled with Zionist idealism, immigrated to Israel in 1965. He moved to a kibbutz where he studied Hebrew, worked, and joined the Israel Defense Forces. As a young journalist in 1971 he witnessed Israel's various conflicts; he started as the military reporter for the *Jerusalem Post* and subsequently became editor-in-chief of the *Jerusalem Report*. Hirsh has been a contributing editor of *US News & World Report*, a contributor to the *New Republic*, and a news analyst for CBS News. As a strategic fellow at the Washington Institute for Near East Policy, he co-authored with W. Seth Carus *The Future Battlefield and the Arab–Israel Conflict*. He has also written an official history of the Israeli navy, and in 2005 published his memoirs, *Let Me Create a Paradise, God Said to Himself: A Journey of Conscience from Johannesburg to Jerusalem*.

Hirsh is married with four children and lives in Jerusalem.

A Homeland Built on Cake

Johannesburg

The Zionist engine in the house was my mom. She was, as was politely said, 'a soldier', or 'a worker' of the Women's Zionist League. She never sought office nor rank in the organisation but when it came to door-to-door collecting from the several dozen Jewish families within a few miles' radius of our home or collecting secondhand clothes for a jumble sale, all the proceeds for the Jewish State, she had no second.

The monthly cake sale took place in the vestibule of the Yeoville Synagogue where the fine ladies of the Jewish community would buy cakes for shillings, not pennies. The night before a sale, the cakes would all be brought to our house where a committee headed by the fabulous Mrs Rappaport, the community beauty who had survived two rich husbands, would decide how much to price each one. One should not underestimate the politics involved. Try charging less for Mrs Spitz's cheesecake than Mrs Hirshbaum's chocolate torte, and surviving. Once priced, these creations would be placed in white square boxes and stacked on the spare bed in my room. Next to them, in straw baskets, sat cellophane bags of homemade sweets, all smelling delicious and tantalisingly close, but remaining secure in that one would never dream of stealing from the Zionist cause. Those bags of sweets and boxes of cake were bricks in the building of our homeland and how proud I was to be part of the effort.

~

With great fanfare came the publication of the famous *New International Goodwill Recipe Book* or the *Yeoville Book* as it is known throughout South Africa. First published in 1950, it contained kosher recipes submitted by the ladies of Johannesburg, all of which, according to my mom, were useless. What Jewish woman, she wanted to know, would give away her most precious culinary secrets in a society where small talk was king and talk about food was almost a religious experience? Why on earth, she wanted to know, would Goldie Fishbein want anyone to make her *teiglach*[1] as well as she did? My mom remained convinced, despite all the proof over the years to the contrary as my sisters and family churned out delicious dish after dish by going according to the book, that the contributors had added a spoon of sugar too much or missed a pinch of salt.

---

1   Pastries boiled in a sweet syrup.

ONE EGG IS A FORTUNE

Those bags of sweets and boxes of cake were bricks in the building of our homeland and how proud I was to be part of the effort.

top left: Hirsh Goodman, aged ten, Johannesburg, South Africa (1956).

top right: Hirsh as an Israeli paratrooper (1967).

above: Overlooking the Red Canyon, south of Eilat, Israel (1965).

left: Hirsh with his son Shai on the day of Shai's induction into the Israeli army (1989).

Israel

It was my first time in an aeroplane and my first time outside South Africa. I had begun as a sapling and now I was a seed on a journey to be replanted in the soil of my own country, my own land, Israel. En route to our kibbutz, at the Nachshon Junction the truck turned off to refuel at a Delek petrol station. We were told that we should stretch our legs, use the toilets, visit the little zoo in the garden out back or stop by Sarah's kiosk, a must-see for the boys. I walked through the zoo quickly, hating to see animals in cages, and then on to the kiosk to buy a *gazoz*, a drink made of syrup and soda water drawn from a silver tap on the counter. The line was long but it had not formed away from the counter, but rather along it for reasons that very soon became apparent.

Sarah, the lady bending over the various tubs of ice-cream filling cones with scoops, had the largest breasts and the lowest-cut shirt I had ever seen. And she knew it. We were later to learn that Sarah was a regional celebrity. Truck-drivers made detours to have a peek and exchange a few naughty but playful words with Sarah of the Nachshon Junction, known universally, and now to us as well, as Sarah Parra – *parra* being a cow. 'Told you this was a land of milk and honey,' I said to my friend.

Adapted from Hirsh Goodman's Let Me Create a Paradise, God Said To Himself: A Journey of Conscience from Johannesburg to Jerusalem *(Public Affairs, 2005) used with permission of Hirsh Goodman.*

Fête Fare
Mini Cheeseless Cheese Cakes
Treats for young and old

BASE
200g Marie or plain sweet biscuits,
  crushed
125g butter, melted

FILLING
3 eggs, separated
1 x 395g tin sweetened condensed milk
2 teaspoons cornflour
½ cup lemon juice

Preheat oven to 150°C. Line a 11cm x 22cm tin or similarly sized container with foil or baking paper.

Make base: Combine ingredients and set aside ¼ of this mixture for the topping. Firmly press mixture evenly over the tin.

Make filling: Beat egg whites until stiff. Combine remaining ingredients in a separate bowl and fold in egg whites. Pour over the base and sprinkle with topping. Bake for 30 minutes and cool. Refrigerate before slicing.
(MAKES APPROX. 20 PIECES)

Recipes for Mini Florentines and Rocky Road – see page 307.

RUTH HENDEL

Ruth Hendel is a Broadway theatre producer.

She was born in Connecticut, USA, the daughter of Abraham and Anne Shapiro Goldberg.

She graduated with a Bachelor of Fine Arts in theatre with honours from the University of Connecticut and earned a Masters degree in communication from Northwestern University.

Her Broadway productions include *Passing Strange, Steel Magnolias, High Fidelity, Legally Blonde, Fela! and Priscilla, Queen of the Desert*. The off-Broadway hit musical *Altar Boyz* continued to play to rave reviews after four years. Ruth won the 2002 Drama Desk Award Outstanding New Play for *Metamorphoses*, the 2003 Drama Desk Award Unique Theatrical Experience, the 2003 Lucille Lortel Award for the off-Broadway *The Exonerated*, and the 2008 Drama Desk Award Outstanding Musical for *Passing Strange*. Ruth's work has been nominated many times for the prestigious Tony Award, and has received the top honour.

Ruth is involved in production tours in the US and supports many not-for-profit theatres. She is a board member and vice-chair of the Eugene O'Neill Theater Center in Waterford, Connecticut; the LAByrinth Theater Company in New York; the Play Company; and the Emelin Theater in Mamaroneck, New York.

In 2006 Ruth received the University of Connecticut's School of Fine Arts alumni award. When not at the theatre, Ruth enjoys cooking, hand-weaving, and volunteering for local schools and charity organisations.

Ruth lives in Connecticut with her husband Stephen. They have three adult children.

Fresh Produce Productions

$\mathcal{B}$ack in the '50s when I was growing up in Norwich, a small southeastern Connecticut town, my family ate at a large round maple table with a revolving lazy Susan in the middle. Our life was centred around that table. Back then, we ate dinner as a family. Six o'clock was dinner time and a square meal was always served. My mother didn't prepare fancy foods but everything was fresh and wholesome. Instinctively, she knew about the healthy food pyramid years before dieticians devised the chart.

My mother also taught me to 'start your kettle in the morning'; in other words, don't wait until the last minute to prepare the meals for the day, buy only fresh produce (even dried spices have to be fresh), start from scratch and never use a mix. And while you're at it, be sure to check for rancid odours, mould and bugs. Fear botulism, lysteria and mayonnaise, but enjoy the food. That's a tall order!

Lifestyles change and when my children were growing up in Westchester, a small suburban town outside of New York City, their busy schedules – little league baseball, soccer, hockey, dance, religious instruction, boy scouts, girl scouts, play dates and so forth – made it very difficult to find time to cook and have family meals, especially during the week. Between chauffeuring and bookings, I somehow managed to get meals on the table even if everyone ate at a different time. Each meal lasted seven minutes times three, but all the food was creatively made and brimming with protein and vitamins (with some sweets thrown in for good measure!).

When it boils down to it, I cook with love. I have an overwhelming desire to nurture and to feed my family and friends. Somehow the years have flown by and my children are now young adults and out of the house. My daily duties at the stove are pretty much over. Do I miss all the meal preparation? No. But I do miss the noise and commotion and making large kettles of soup for my family. Feeding my children was my way of expressing love. My husband is easy to please and we eat out more than we should. Our nest is empty.

So what do I do with all my pent-up love? My 'nuturing neuroses'? I burst with excitement anticipating holidays knowing my family will be together. All my love and energy is fueled into one big get-together. I long for our annual 4th of July picnic when I make delicious potato salad to the delight of my son Sam; if only Thanksgiving came twice a year so I could please my daughter Abby and make her favourite stuffing; or every night be a *Rosh Hashanah* dinner so I can watch my youngest son Joe enjoy the brisket. Basically, I make a huge production out

ONE EGG IS A FORTUNE

Ruth with her husband Stephen.

of everything. I want to make all the traditional dishes that go along with each holiday. I want to please each child, in-laws and friends with food and love. I even want to please my sister-in-law's father-in-law who loves my traditional sweet potato *tzimmes*. I know it's crazy – but it's who I am.

Many years ago, I fell into a new career producing plays and musicals on Broadway and off-Broadway. My first play was Mary Zimmerman's *Metamorphoses*. It turned out to be a hit. More than twenty other productions have followed, such as Tony Kushner's *Caroline, or Change* and Lorraine Hansberry's *A Raisin in the Sun* starring Sean Combs (P. Diddy). I often say that I went from brisket to Broadway. Do you think that could be a title of a new musical?

I've incorporated my cooking/love craze in my theatre world. I invite my 'new' theatre family to enjoy the holidays with my relatives. I get to be the lead producer (star/diva all in one). I cast the show (pick out the menu); I do costumes (I wear my nicest apron always in sync with the specific holiday); I'm the scenic designer (set the table); I light the show (with candles); and then as all good producers do, I entice a hungry audience of family and friends to come and have fun and eat. I am a happy producer! I reap royalties in the form of leftovers.

And although I've often thought of calling my production company Fresh Produce, for the time being I'll just stick with Ruth Hendel Productions. I have to have some secrets.

My mother also taught me to 'start your kettle in the morning'; in other words, don't wait until the last minute to prepare the meals for the day, buy only fresh produce (even dried spices have to be fresh), start from scratch and never use a mix.

Lemon Angel Cake

As a Broadway theatre producer, I am an angel of sorts –

9 eggs
¾ cup caster sugar
¾ cup sifted plain flour (potato or rice
    flour can be substituted to make
    gluten-free)
1½ teaspoons grated lemon zest
1 tablespoon lemon juice
¼ cup extra caster sugar
lemon icing
candied citrus strips, optional
pashmak (also known as Persian fairy
    floss), optional

LEMON ICING
4½ cups icing sugar
3–4 tablespoons fresh lemon juice

CANDIED CITRUS STRIPS
1 medium orange
1 medium lemon
1 cup (220g) caster sugar
½ cup (125ml) water
extra white sugar

Make candied citrus strips: Peel fruit carefully and slice peel into very fine strips, about ½cm x 3cm. Combine sugar and water, stir over low heat until sugar dissolves. Add peel, simmering for about 10 minutes, stirring occasionally to prevent burning. Remove peel, drain slightly, toss in crystal sugar. Put peel on a wire rack until thoroughly dry, overnight for or at least 12 hours. Store in an airtight container.

Preheat oven to 180°C.

Make cake: Separate eggs; place **8 yolks** into large mixing bowl and **9 whites** into a separate bowl. Beat egg yolks until light and pale yellow in colour. Add sugar and continue beating until very thick and creamy (approx. 10 minutes). Add flour, lemon zest and juice until well-blended. Beat egg whites until they begin to stiffen. Slowly add extra sugar and continue to beat until it resembles a stiff meringue.

Using a spatula, gently fold the egg whites into the cake batter. Pour mixture into an **ungreased** 23cm angel-cake or chiffon tin, smooth the top, and bake for 35–40 minutes, until it springs back to the touch. Remove cake from the oven and immediately invert the tin onto its feet on a flat surface. When the cake has cooled to room temperature, run a sharp knife around the edge of the tin and along the centre tube. Turn the cake out.

Make icing: Combine ingredients and pour over the top of cake, allowing the icing to drizzle down the sides. If using citrus slices and/or *pashmak*, decorate just before serving. To store, wrap well and do not refrigerate.

Note: The un-iced cake freezes very well.

(SERVES 12)

Martin Indyk
is an American
diplomat
and expert on
Middle Eastern
affairs.

MARTIN
INDYK

His parents John and Mary left their native Poland before World War II as children.

Martin was born in 1951 in London, England, around the time that his father was completing postgraduate studies in surgery. The family immigrated to Australia and Martin gained an economics degree from the University of Sydney in 1972 and a PhD in international relations from the Australian National University in Canberra in 1977.

In 1982 Martin migrated to the United States and worked as a deputy research director for AIPAC (American Israel Public Affairs Committee) followed by eight years' service as the founding executive director of the Washington Institute for Near East Policy. He was appointed adjunct professor at the John Hopkins School of Advanced International Studies, teaching at the Middle East Institute at Columbia University, Tel Aviv University in Israel, and Macquarie University in Sydney.

Diplomatic service has been manifold. Martin was the US ambassador to Israel from 1995–97 and from 2000–01. Before that he served as special assistant to the then US president Bill Clinton, in the US National Security Council, and as senior director of Near East and South Asia Affairs. From 1997–2000 he served as assistant secretary of state for Near East Affairs under Madeleine Albright. He played an important role on Clinton's Middle East peace team and was the White House representative on the US–Israel Science and Technology Commission. Martin is currently a Senior Fellow and Director of the Saban Center for Middle East Policy at the Brookings Institution in Washington, DC.

Martin has published widely on the topics of US policy regarding the Arab–Israeli peace process, US–Israeli relations and current Iraq and Iran issues. His book *Innocent Abroad: An Intimate Account of American Peace Diplomacy in the Middle East* was published in January 2009.

Martin has two children, Sarah and Jacob.

Lili's Strudel

My friendship with Arik (Ariel) Sharon goes back many years. Sharon became prime minister of Israel in 2001 during my second stint as US ambassador to Israel. In the same year Joan Nathan, an internationally acclaimed expert on food, published her cookbook *The Foods of Israel Today*, a compilation of recipes and stories from varied ethnic backgrounds. Some of the recipes were named after personalities such as 'Chief of Staff Cholent', in honour of Amnon Lipkin-Shachak, the former chief of staff and politician. I was very excited to see Arik's late wife Lili's wonderful cooking included.

To launch the book, the US embassy hosted a luncheon for Joan and the contributors. Colin, the chef-in-residence, prepared a feast using as many recipes from the book as possible. Lili's strudel was one of them. I remember this strudel very well because she always used to serve it when I visited Sharon's ranch at the gate to the Negev Desert. Their home was continually filled with people and Lili's love of cooking was evident by their table always groaning with food. Arik was a big eater. He loved food, especially Lili's home cooking.

Prior to a scheduled appointment to meet with Arik and the director of the CIA, Jill, my wife at the time, thought it would be nice to prepare the strudel for him. Colin, our chef, baked it according to Joan Nathan's recipe and Jill wrapped it in cellophane. A few minutes before the meeting, I presented my gift to Arik – the strudel with a copy of the cookbook. He was speechless and didn't know quite how to respond. Lili had passed away a year earlier. Arik was visibly choked up. He was a man who did not usually display his emotions. I showed him Lili's contribution and her photograph alongside. He looked at it for a while and read it. He picked up the phone and called his two sons Omri and Gilad into his office. Pointing to the gifts, he said, 'Look, the ambassador has brought me your mother's strudel. Take a look at this; your mother's in a book that has been published in America!'

By coincidence, it was Arik's granddaughter's birthday that day and he declared that Lili's strudel would be part of their celebration that night.

Morello Cherry Strudel

In honour of Lili Sharon

FILLING

1 jar (approx. 700g) morello cherries, stoned and drained

½ cup sugar

½ cup breadcrumbs

1 tablespoon unsalted butter

PASTRY

6 sheets filo dough, defrosted and covered with damp cloth to prevent drying

¼ cup melted unsalted butter

4 tablespoons sugar

4 tablespoons ground almonds

icing sugar, for serving

Preheat oven to 180°C. Line a baking tray with baking paper.

Make filling: Sprinkle cherries with sugar and set aside. Heat butter in a small pan, add breadcrumbs and stir until golden. Remove from heat and set aside.

Prepare pastry: Mix sugar and almonds in a bowl. Lay 1 sheet of filo dough on a flat surface or board. Brush with melted butter and sprinkle with about 1½ tablespoons sugar and almond mixture. Top with a second sheet of filo and repeat the process until you have 6 layers. Sprinkle fried breadcrumbs evenly over the pastry. Spread the cherry filling along one long side and roll up, tuck ends under to enclose.

Place strudel on baking tray, seam side down. Brush top with remaining melted butter. Lay a piece of extra baking paper over top of strudel. Bake for 20 minutes and remove extra baking paper. Bake for a further 15 minutes until golden. Cool before serving. Dust with icing sugar.

(SERVES 8; MAKES 1 STRUDEL)

Rachael Kohn is
a multi-award-
winning producer
and broadcaster,
author and speaker
on religion and
spirituality.

RACHAEL KOHN

The youngest of three, she was born in 1953 in Toronto, Canada. Her parents Stephen and Jana and her sister Helen were born in Czechoslovakia and her other sister Ilana was born in Jerusalem.

Rachael received a Bachelor of Arts in religious studies and sociology from Concordia University, and both a Masters and a PhD in religious studies from McMaster University. She was awarded the Leverhulme Post-Doctoral Fellowship from the University of Lancaster.

After moving to Australia, Rachael lectured in religious studies and Semitic studies at the University of Sydney. In 2005, she also received the degree *Doctor of Letters honoris causa* from the University of NSW. In 1992 Rachael joined the ABC's Radio National.

Rachael has won many international awards for radio and television documentaries, including *The Dead Sea Scrolls* and *Buddhism East and West*. She has won the World Gold Medal three times for *In God We Trust: Civil and Uncivil Religion in America* (2000), *Coffee, Sex and Other Addictions: New Age Health in the 19th Century* (2002) and *The Monk and the Modern Girl: A Journey into China's Past and Present* (2004). She has interviewed many people from diverse religious and ethnic backgrounds including the Dalai Lama, V.S. Naipaul and Elie Wiesel.

Her books, *The New Believers: Re-Imagining God* and *Curious Obsessions in the History of Religion and Science*, are indicative of Rachael's passion for spirituality and religion. She has also written widely for academic publications and the press, including *Learning from History: Pre-War Germany and Now* published by the Council of Christians and Jews in 2007.

Rachael currently produces and presents *The Spirit of Things* and *The Ark* on Radio National. She regularly addresses a wide array of organisations on the contemporary issues of spiritual and religious values.

Rachael lives with her husband Tom in Sydney.

Untold Sensory Delights

As postwar immigrants to Canada, life for my parents was measured in long work days. We had no relatives to speak of and as children we saw our parents for short snatches in the morning and evening. It was a great delight to spend rare time alone with my mother, especially when we went to the Jewish market towards the end of the week.

The Jewish market, also known as Kensington Market, was the oldest Jewish enclave of Toronto, and it continues to have a place in Canadian Jewish history books. Its old criss-crossed streets and laneways of Jewish shops offered untold sensory delights. To me, nothing in the world compared to the sweet yeasty smell of Lottman's Bakery where the smiling ladies behind the counter would never let me leave without a cookie. The cheese shops were experiences in gigantism with everything on display a hundred times the normal supermarket size – huge hunks of butter, giant wheels of cheese, and my favourite blocks of chocolate-marbled halva. The delicatessens could be sniffed a block away, with their mandatory large barrels of pickles and smoked herring, two of the most wonderful smells imaginable. When I was a teenager, one pickle-seller convinced me that if I climbed up on a barrel in the back room, I would get the best pickles in the house, which I obediently did, only to realise it wasn't that sort of pickle he was referring to. I especially loved watching the Italian fruiterers yelling out lower and lower prices as they competed for customers. I am sure that's where I was hardwired in the art of getting a bargain.

The best part of the shopping day was always the last stop, Lottman's Bakery, where no matter what my mother chose, it was bound to please. It also meant that we were drawing closer to a special time of the day, when we would return home and have a snack of twisted poppy-seed buns (which we called *hoski*) with smoked herring. It was followed, after a decent interval, with tea and one of the sublime baked sweets, which could have included poppy-seed roll, chocolate-filled yeast *kugelhupf*, or *kolace*, a specialty of the Czech kitchen.

The Jewish market is now only a fragrant memory to ageing Torontonians. Subsequent migrant waves of Italians, Portuguese, West Indians and Chinese have replaced the Jewish shop-owners. My last memories of it are from the early 1970s when I was a college student. I cycled there every week, hoping somehow to stave off its inevitable disappearance, as sons and daughters of the retailers aspired to the professions, like I did, leaving behind the family business.

Buchti: 'Little Pillows'
Food for angels

'My sisters and I would devour four of five of these little pillows at a time. I often think of how despairing my mother must have felt after all that work, to be left with only a few for her coffee.'

DOUGH
15g fresh yeast (5½ teaspoons dried yeast)
pinch salt
55g caster sugar
1 cup milk
2 eggs, 1 whole and 1 yolk
100g unsalted butter, melted
1¾ cups plain flour
½ lemon, rind grated
plain flour, for dusting and rolling
extra 100g unsalted butter, melted
icing sugar, for dusting

POPPY SEED FILLING*
1 ⅓ cups (300g) ground poppy seeds
2 cups milk
½ cup sultanas
⅔ cup sugar, or more to taste

CREAM CHEESE FILLING*
500g farm (curd) cheese
1 egg, beaten
⅔ cup caster sugar
½ cup icing sugar
½ lemon, rind grated
½ cup sultanas (optional)
apricot jam or *povidl* plum jam (optional)

*This recipe has 2 suggested fillings; halve the filling ingredients if using both.

Make dough: Heat the milk until tepid. Mix yeast, salt and a teaspoon of sugar in a small bowl until creamy. Stir in half a cup of the milk and set aside for 5–10 minutes to froth. In another bowl, whisk eggs, butter and remaining sugar and milk. Place flour in a large bowl and make a well in the centre. Pour in egg and yeast mixtures, add lemon rind and beat with a wooden spoon until dough comes away from sides. Dust with flour, cover with a clean, dry cloth, and leave in a warm place to double in bulk (about 1 hour).

Make poppy seed filling: Combine all ingredients in a small saucepan, bring to the boil, then simmer for about 30 minutes until a thick paste forms. The filling must not be too wet. Set aside and cool.

Make cream cheese filling: Combine all ingredients in a bowl and set aside.

Make buchti: Preheat oven to 180°C. Grease sides of a cake tin or baking dish (approx. 25cm x 30cm) and dust with plain flour. Roll out dough on a lightly floured surface until 5mm thick. Cut into 6cm squares and place a teaspoon of filling into the centre of each; if using cream cheese filling, a little jam may be placed next to the cheese. Pull in the corners of the dough, pinching them together. Place each round 'pillow' upside down in the baking dish next to each other, touching sides. Brush each bun with melted butter. Cover with a cloth and leave to rise for another 30 minutes. Bake for about 25 minutes, until golden, and turn out as a whole onto a cooling rack. Separate the buns when cool. Sprinkle with icing sugar.

(MAKES 40 YEAST BUNS)

Madeleine Kunin
is a diplomat,
politician
and academic.

MADELEINE
KUNIN

She was born in 1933 in Zurich, Switzerland, and migrated to the United States in 1940. Her grandparents were born in Alsace, France.

Madeleine completed tertiary studies at the University of Massachusetts, Columbia University Graduate School of Journalism, and the University of Vermont and has received numerous honorary degrees. Before commencing her political career, she worked as a journalist at Burlington Free Press, as a tour guide at the World's Fair, and as a part-time college professor.

Madeleine is a former Vermont state legislator (1972–78), lieutenant-governor (1978–82) and governor of Vermont (1985–91; three terms). She was the first female governor of Vermont and the first US Jewish governor. Madeleine was the first woman in US history to be elected governor three times. Focusing on the environment, education and children's issues, she also initiated the family court system. She was appointed the first woman to the State Supreme Court. From 1993 to 1996 she served as US deputy secretary of education in the Clinton administration. From 1996 to 1999, Madeleine was the United States ambassador to Switzerland and Liechtenstein. Having an understanding of the culture enabled Madeleine to negotiate positive discussions regarding the Jewish assets and gold stolen by the Nazis during World War II.

Madeleine lectures in women's politics and runs leadership seminars at the University of Vermont. She continues to be involved in community activities, particularly in the area of women's rights, child welfare and health, and literature. She is the author of *The Big Green Book*, *Living a Political Life* and *Pearls, Politics and Power: How Women Can Win and Lead*.

Madeleine lives in Burlington, Vermont, with her husband John Hennessey. She has four children and five grandchildren.

Dinner at the White House

I remember my first dinner at the White House; how thrilling it was! Although I had been invited to attend hundreds of formal dinners during my years in public office, this is still the one that has left the strongest impression.

Over the years the White House has been renovated and refurbished to incorporate the needs of each administration, including many of the formal rooms used for receptions, luncheons, and larger official dinners for visiting heads of state.

President and Mrs Carter planned special occasions to entertain visiting heads of state, members of Congress, state governors and other dignitaries. Each event was carefully orchestrated to reflect the tastes and interests of the guests with elaborate well-thought-out menus, table decorations and music. Although Jimmy Carter had banned hard liquor, wine was still offered. One of the social events of the annual Governors' Conference was an invitation to dine at the White House with the president followed by entertainment in the East Room.

This very first dinner was intimate with only thirteen guests and yet it was still a black-tie occasion. I felt really nervous. Would I use the right fork? Would I drink from the correct crystal glass?

The dinner took place during the final term of the Carter administration, which was dominated by the Iran hostage crisis. The United States was struggling to rescue diplomats and American citizens held in Tehran. With his administration drawing to a close and popularity sagging, Carter decided that dialogue with people from different parts of the country – mayors and city officials – could shed light on this difficult crisis. I was lieutenant-governor of Vermont at the time.

On arrival we were asked to wait in the library, a beautiful and peaceful room with books lining the walls and a painting of George Washington above the fireplace. Several other guests arrived and were also ushered into the library. One of them was Ed Koch, the mayor of New York. He turned to my husband at the time and asked, 'And what city are you mayor of?' The assumption was obvious – that my husband was the important official and I was just the spouse!

Being such a small gathering, we managed to have a private dialogue with the president. Other issues were discussed, including the Panama Canal Treaty that was being ratified by the Congress. Again he was having difficulty with support and votes and he talked about what he had to do to win approval from the Senate. All in all, it was an extraordinary evening.

French Apple Tarte
Our much-loved classic

'My grandmother came from Alsace, France. This is her recipe that was handed down to my mother and then on to me.'

PASTRY
60g butter
2 tablespoons white sugar
1 egg, lightly beaten
1 cup plain flour, sifted
½ teaspoon baking powder
pinch of salt
extra flour, for rolling dough

FILLING
1 egg
3 tablespoons white sugar
⅓ cup single cream
3 cooking apples such as Granny Smith, peeled, cored and thinly sliced

Preheat oven to 180°C. Line a 20cm non-stick spring form tin with baking paper.

Make pastry: Cream butter and sugar until light and fluffy. Add the egg and then flour, baking powder and salt. Turn out onto a lightly floured surface, knead gently and roll out to form a thin pastry to cover the base and sides of the tin.

Make filling: Arrange the apple slices in an overlapping spiral pattern in the tin. Beat the egg, sugar and cream together until thick and pour over the apples. Press the apples gently down into the mixture. Bake for approximately 30–45 minutes until set.
(SERVES 8)

Fresh Apple Kuchen

WALNUT TOPPING
⅓ cup walnuts, chopped
½ cup caster sugar
2 teaspoons ground cinnamon

CAKE
3 eggs

¾ cup caster sugar
⅓ cup vegetable oil
¾ cup superfine plain flour (or *matzo* meal)
5 cooking apples such as Granny Smith, peeled, cored and thinly sliced

Preheat oven to 180°C. Line the base of a 20 or 23cm spring form tin with baking paper and grease the sides of the tin.

Make the walnut topping: Combine all the ingredients and set aside.

Make the cake: Beat eggs and sugar until light and creamy. Gradually add the oil and flour and beat well. To make the first layer, pour half the mixture into tin and arrange half the apples evenly on top. To make the second layer, repeat the process. Sprinkle topping over the apples. Bake for 1 hour and 10 minutes. Allow to cool before turning out.
(SERVES 8)

Isi Leibler AO CBE is a prominent Jewish leader and human rights advocate.

ISI AND NAOMI LEIBLER

He was born in 1934 in Antwerp, Belgium, and migrated to Melbourne, Australia, with his parents just before the outbreak of World War II. He studied political science and sociology at the University of Melbourne.

In 1958, Isi married Naomi Porush, the daughter of Rebbitzin Bertha and Rabbi Dr Israel Porush, chief rabbi of the Great Synagogue in Sydney. Naomi was born in London in 1937 and migrated to Australia with her family in June 1940. She was president of B'nai B'rith Young Women, president of the Sydney University Jewish Students' Union, and vice-president of the National Union of Australasian Jewish Students. Naomi has been deeply involved in Isi's communal activities.

Starting out in the travel industry in 1965, Isi's company Jetset Tours became Australia's largest travel organisation with branches in Asia, North America and Europe.

Isi is deeply committed to the Australian and international Jewish community. His positions have included vice-president, chairman of the governing board, and senior vice-president of the World Jewish Congress. He was a founding member of the international movement to save Soviet Jewry and helped to secure their liberation.

Isi has also worked to foster relations between Asia–Pacific nations and world Jewry. His meetings with senior Indian and Chinese officials helped accelerate diplomatic relations between Israel and these countries.

He was awarded a Commander of Order of the British Empire in 1977, an Officer of the Order of Australia in 1989, and an honorary Doctor of Letters from Deakin University in 1990.

Isi and Naomi immigrated to Israel in 1999 and live in Jerusalem. Isi is a regular contributor to the *Jerusalem Post* and Naomi is world president of Emunah, the Women's Religious Zionist Organisation. They have one daughter, three sons, and many grandchildren.

Miracle in Moscow

One Friday night we will never ever forget...

Isi and I became involved with the plight of Soviet Jewry in the early 1960s, long before it was taken up worldwide. Our first visit to Russia was in 1978; the Soviets finally granted us a visa because Isi's travel agency Jetset was associated with the 1980 Moscow Olympic Games. It was the first of many such trips.

In 1985, Mikhail Gorbachev introduced the policy of *glasnost* (openness) which extended people's freedoms and opened up internal debate in the country's political system.

Each time we visited Russia we had the opportunity to meet many wonderful people. Once, the chief rabbi of Russia invited us to spend *Rosh Hashanah* and *Yom Kippur* in Moscow with him. After a number of visits, we developed close relationships with many *refuseniks* – people denied permission to emigrate abroad.

The Friday night we will never forget took place in February 1989 in Moscow. After opening the Solomon Mikhoels Center – the first Jewish cultural centre to be allowed in seventy years, named after the renowned Jewish actor murdered by Stalin – we hosted a *Shabbat* meal at our luxury hotel. *Refuseniks* had been too frightened to set foot inside this hotel prior to this evening. We didn't have a large room, but we'd invited twelve to fourteen people to join us for dinner. We'd arrived in Russia with suitcases packed with kosher food – canned goods, packets of *gefilte* fish balls, instant soups and vacuum-packed cold cuts. We also brought plastic plates, cups, cutlery; literally everything bar the kitchen sink! We supplemented these supplies by visiting the local market and buying lettuce, limited raw vegetables and apples.

But word had spread amongst our *refusenik* friends and over thirty people crowded into our small room. Panic stations! How to feed thirty people with barely enough food for fourteen? Solution: cut every piece of fish in half! There weren't enough chairs, so some sat on the floor. Everyone ate something, no one went hungry. Dudu Fisher, the well-known Israeli singer, sang traditional Sabbath songs that were known throughout the world.

It was an incredibly moving experience for all who attended. For an event like this to take place so openly in those days was in itself a miracle.

Honey Glace Slice

To wish everyone a sweet year

LIGHT HONEY CAKE

1 cup plain flour
1 cup self-raising flour
½ teaspoon bicarbonate of soda
1 teaspoon cinnamon
½ teaspoon instant coffee powder
½ tablespoon cocoa
2 eggs
1 cup caster sugar
½ cup vegetable oil
250g honey
1 cup boiling water

glace or ice-cream (or non-dairy substitute)
1½ litre vanilla ice-cream, slightly softened at room temperature

BUTTERSCOTCH SAUCE

¾ cup brown sugar
½ cup golden syrup
6 tablespoons unsalted butter or 4 tablespoons margarine
¼ cup caster sugar
pinch salt
few drops vanilla essence
½ cup cream or non-dairy cream
honeycomb pieces, for decoration

Make honey cake: Preheat oven at 180°C. Grease a square 20cm tin and line with baking paper. Sift flours, bicarbonate, cinnamon, coffee and cocoa together. In a separate bowl, beat eggs and gradually add sugar. When mixture is light and fluffy, slowly add oil, then honey and finally dry ingredients, making sure the flour is completely absorbed. Slowly add the boiling water, mix well and pour into the cake tin. Bake for about 45 minutes, until a skewer inserted comes out clean. Allow the cake to cool in the tin.

Make butterscotch sauce: Place all ingredients except cream into a saucepan. Bring to the boil, reduce heat and simmer until thickened, about 5 minutes. Remove from heat, stir in cream and set aside to cool. Reheat just before serving.

To assemble: Turn cold cake out onto a flat surface. Using a very sharp knife, cut the cake horizontally in half. Cut off any uneven pieces on the top of each half to ensure the cake surface is flat. Wash and dry the cake tin and line again with baking paper. Place one half of the cake back into the tin and gently spread it evenly with the softened ice-cream. Place the second cake layer on top, pushing it down gently. Cover with plastic wrap and set in freezer until ready to serve. Cut the cake into small squares. Place a square into a dessert bowl and pour a small quantity of sauce over the top. Decorate with honeycomb pieces.

(SERVES 16)

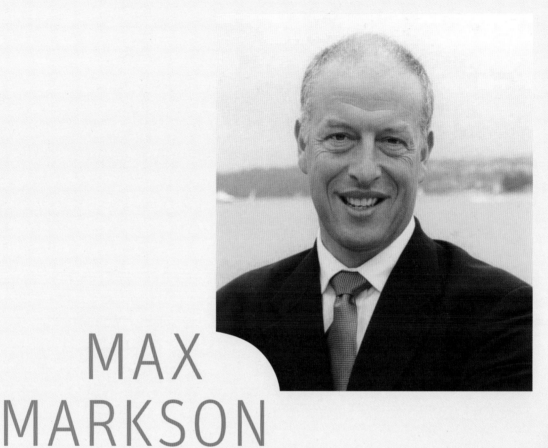

MAX MARKSON

Max Markson specialises in public relations, celebrity management and event organisation.

He was born in 1956 in Bournemouth, United Kingdom, the son of Leon and Stella. His grandparents came from eastern Europe.

From the age of five, Max worked behind the scenes of his father's business, the *Leon Markson Aquashow,* which toured the UK and Europe. For nine years, it gave him the opportunity to learn about the entertainment industry.

Max's first business venture began on a holiday in Australia in September 1977 during the federal election campaign. When money ran short, he sold T-shirts printed with the image of the two prime ministerial candidates.

Max is sometimes referred to as a publicity machine. His career in PR evolved from promoting pop groups, BBC Radio 1 DJs, running a discothèque called The Zoo, working at the radio station 2WS and organising wet T-shirt competitions. His own PR company, Markson-Sparks, was established in 1982.

Today Max manages celebrities and sports personalities. He has arranged over 200 fundraising dinners, giving over $40 million to charity, with special guests including Bill Clinton, George Bush Senior, Nelson Mandela, Rudy Giuliani and Al Gore.

Max's book, *Show Me The Money,* details the first forty years of his life. Max has two daughters and lives in Sydney, Australia.

Confessions of a Chocoholic

I have a very sweet tooth and I am a self-confessed chocoholic. Indeed, my love of chocolate and ice-cream borders on addiction. Some people go on pub-crawls; I satisfy my palate with chocolate and ice-cream crawls.

My publicity work has allowed me to indulge in my passion for ice-cream and chocolate. I promoted the launch of the sixth Norgen-Vaaz outlet and then every other store until there was a chain of 63 outlets. The concept was simple: get a celebrity to eat ice-cream. You would be surprised how many ways that can be done, from blindfolded ice-cream tastings to celebrities arriving in Rolls-Royces. One of the best was when Mount Everest climber Tim McCartney-Snape abseiled down the side of a building eating an ice-cream. We launched all of Norgen - Vaaz's new flavours with special deliveries to every TV and radio host in the country.

There are few pleasures as sensual as eating fine chocolate. I have dreamt of opening up a chain of chocolate cafés all over the world like Starbucks and Max Brenner. There must be something in the name Max! Sydney also boasts the world's first Lindt chocolate concept store and café in the centre of the city.

Can you guess the theme for one of my birthday celebrations? Chocolate, of course! Because the party was in my honour, only chocolate-based creations were served.

I host many functions and promote people and products in Australia and abroad. In 1985 I met Anthea Leonard from Sweet Art in Paddington, NSW, a genius who can turn a cake into a work of art. Anthea created a birthday face cake for my friend, the author Tom Keneally; it was surrounded by the covers of his books and was so good, he just couldn't bring himself to cut it. On another occasion we arranged for Anthea's work to be sponsored by the Australian bakery Top Taste, promoting the Australia Day celebrations. She baked fifteen fruitcakes, all decorated with the faces of famous Aussies: Olivia Newton-John and Bob Hawke amongst them. The cakes were on public display for six weeks, then we took them on the road to shopping centres for a few months. At a media presentation, Bob Hawke's nose broke off and Anthea whipped out her instant emergency first-aid kit; with a bit of cream and icing, no-one would have known otherwise – except that this fix was the front page photo for the *Daily Telegraph*.

I enjoy being involved in the planning stages of events, especially the dessert menus. At a private dinner for the former mayor of New York, Rudy Giuliani, a delicious cinnamon ice-cream with a chocolate fudge brownie cake was served. Memorable!

My dentist and fitness trainer will *love* reading this!

Adapted from Max Markson's Show Me The Money *(Viking, Penguin Books Australia, 2000) used with permission of Max Markson.*

Toblerone Chocolate Mousse

Pure decadence and family favourite

6 x 200g Toblerone milk chocolate blocks
200ml thickened cream (good quality
such as King Island)
6 eggs, separated

Break up the chocolate, melt over a double boiler and then allow to cool slightly. Beat the cream until just stiff. In a separate bowl, beat the whites until stiff. Lightly beat the egg yolks, stir in the melted chocolate and gently stir in the cream. Finally fold in the egg whites. Pour into individual shot glasses, ramekins or in a decorative glass bowl. Refrigerate until set.

Note: To make Toblerone White Chocolate Mousse, substitute milk chocolate with Toblerone white chocolate.

(SERVES 10–12)

MARLEE MATLIN

Marlee Matlin is an Academy Award-winning American movie and television actress.

She was born in 1965 in Morton Grove, Illinois, the daughter of Don and Libby. As a result of a viral infection at the age of eighteen months, Marlee lost most of her hearing, leaving her almost completely deaf. Her parents were determined that Marlee would grow up with the same opportunities as her siblings and peers.

She started acting at the age of seven as Dorothy in a children's theatre version of *The Wizard of Oz*. Her stage production of *Children of a Lesser God* led to her role in the 1986 film, and at age 21 Marlee became the youngest recipient of the Best Actress Oscar and was also honoured with the Golden Globe Award for Best Actress in a Drama.

Marlee has played many roles in television programs including *Reasonable Doubts*, *The West Wing*, *Picket Fences*, *Seinfeld*, *Law and Order* and *Desperate Housewives*. She has also appeared in a number of educational and children's programs including the *Baby Einstein* series, teaching sign language to infants and toddlers, and *Sesame Street*.

Marlee published a novel for children entitled *Deaf Child Crossing* based on her childhood and followed this with the sequel, *Nobody's Perfect*.

She is involved with numerous charitable organisations, including the Children Affected by AIDS Foundation, Elizabeth Glaser Paediatric AIDS Foundation, the Starlight Children's Foundation, and Red Cross Celebrity Cabinet.

Marlee is married to Kevin Grandalski and they have four children.

Flying Out the Kitchen

When I first got married I was determined to be a great cook for my husband. As a police officer, he would come home ravenous after a tough day at work. In between travelling out of town for work or getting up at 4 am to be at the studio at 5, I would do my best to create something other than just chicken on the grill. It worked for a while until we had our first child Sarah; then everything changed.

Kids will eat just about everything when they're young but as they get older they seem to demand creativity on mom and dad's part. 'No onions but I'll eat broccoli' they'll say as they push away their plate. So you try and come up with creative ways to liven up the menu just to get them to eat something other than French fries.

Suddenly, out of necessity, I became fearless and tried out new food combinations. Anything that smacked of 'been there, done that' wasn't going to fly with the kids. Don't misunderstand me, they weren't spoiled. They were just taking after good old Mom. Innovation was the key to keeping them engaged and I quickly learned that the new and original had to be newer and more original than ever.

One day I happened upon my oatmeal cookie recipe that the kids loved, and without even a blink, I improvised it and added something new just as I was doing with every recipe. I simply put in chocolate chips, something I'd seen another parent do with a different cookie recipe. I knew I'd happened upon something when I noticed that the batch I'd just baked was gone within two hours. The choc chips became my secret! And not only were the kids snatching them up, my friends and neighbours were demanding 'Marlee's secret chocolate oatmeal cookies'. Seems adults get bored with the same old food just as kids do!

So I began baking them at lightning speed only to see them fly out of the kitchen even faster. Demand got so high that my chocolate oatmeal cookies had to appear at every occasion and every special holiday, otherwise pandemonium would ensue. And it wasn't a passing fancy or phase. These cookies were here to stay. I'd happened upon something that Mrs Field's Cookies, a popular brand in the United States, discovered a long while back. I'd found a new cookie brand and it was destined to last. Now if I could only figure out a way to get them to eat onions ...

PS: As you can see I call them 'secret'. Kids love anything to do with a secret and the name of the recipe made kids (and adults) want them more! Maybe I should have been in sales ... Ha!

Marlee's Secret Oatmeal Chocolate Chip Cookies

Always a treat

'My husband and kids like to eat these while they are still warm!'

1 cup (220g) butter or margarine (butter makes a better cookie)
1 cup brown sugar, firmly packed
½ cup white sugar (not caster)
1 teaspoon vanilla
2 eggs, lightly beaten
1½ cups plain flour
1 teaspoon bicarbonate of soda (baking soda)
1 teaspoon cinnamon
½ teaspoon salt (optional)
3 cups uncooked oatmeal (such as Quaker Oats)
1 cup chocolate chips

Preheat oven to 180°C. Blend butter and sugars until creamy. Add vanilla and eggs and beat well. Combine flour, bicarbonate of soda, cinnamon and salt in a bowl and stir into the butter mixture. Add oatmeal and chocolate chips. Mix well.

Drop rounded teaspoonfuls onto ungreased baking tray sheet. Bake 10–12 minutes or until golden brown. Remove from oven and allow to cool for 1 minute before placing on a wire rack.

Note: For higher altitudes, for all you mountain goats out there, mix in 1¾ cups flour instead of 1½ cups.

(MAKES 48 COOKIES)

Itamar Rabinovich
is an academic,
diplomat and
author.

ITAMAR
RABINOVICH

He was born in 1942 in Jerusalem, the son of Gutman and Tova. He received a Bachelor of Arts from the Hebrew University of Jerusalem, a Master of Arts from Tel Aviv University, and was awarded a PhD from the University of California. Itamar served in the Israel Defense Forces from 1963–69, holding the rank of lieutenant-colonel.

Having been a member of Tel Aviv University faculty since 1971, Itamar completed an eight-year term as the university's president, served as chairman of the department of Middle Eastern studies, director of the Dayan Center for Middle Eastern and African Studies, dean of humanities and rector. Between 1992 and 1996 he took leave from Tel Aviv University and served as Israel's ambassador to the United States and as chief negotiator with Syria under the late Yitzhak Rabin.

Itamar is the author of several books including *Syria Under the Ba'th*, *The War for Lebanon: 1970– 1985* and *Waging Peace: Israel and the Arabs at the End of the Century*. His latest book, *The View from Damascus*, was published in 2008. He also publishes essays, articles for journals and chapters in books.

Itamar has held public and private positions in Israel and internationally. He has been chairman on several advisory boards and a visiting lecturer in many academic institutions in the US and Canada. He was appointed Charles and Andrea Bronfman Distinguished Fellow at the Saban Center, Brookings Institution, and is a Distinguished Global Professor at New York University. While on sabbatical leave from Tel Aviv University, he was a visiting professor at Harvard's Kennedy School of Government.

In 2004, the French government awarded Itamar the Commandeur de l'Ordre des Palmes Académiques in recognition of his services to education, and in 2007 he received the Grand Decoration in Gold for services to the Republic of Austria.

Itamar and his wife Efrat live in Israel. They have two children and grandchildren.

Coffee as a Peace Offering

In July 1992, the late Yitzhak Rabin appointed me Israel's chief negotiator with Syria. As I was being briefed about the state of the negotiations over the previous few months, I soon found out that it hadn't been much of a negotiation.

The parties had met in a conference room of the State Department for very stiff sessions; the meetings lasted from ten to thirteen hours with a coffee break in the middle. The Syrian delegation refused to shake hands with the Israeli delegation, arguing that one does not shake hands with the enemy. When the time came for coffee breaks, the Syrians would dash out of the room to have coffee in another office. They would not be caught breaking bread or sharing a cup of coffee with 'the enemy'.

Needless to say, in diplomacy substance is the main issue but atmospherics and gestures have their own significance. I realised that in order to break the ice, symbolic steps needed to be taken as well. At my daughter's suggestion I arrived at our first meeting with a bag of Elite Turkish coffee in my briefcase. At the end of my opening statement, I offered my hand to my Syrian counterpart. He shook it. Some ninety minutes later, as the time came for the coffee break, I asked my Syrian counterpart what he thought of the State Department's coffee. 'Not much,' was the answer. 'How about having Middle Eastern coffee?' I asked as I removed the Turkish coffee from my briefcase.

It took the Syrian delegation a few seconds to respond positively and some of the ice was thus broken. This positive response reflected a realisation on the part of the Syrians that the formation of the Rabin government represented a new approach to the peace process. But a bag of Turkish coffee provided the opportunity to translate a new mood into palpable progress.

Choc Prune Pecan Log

Simply mouthwatering

250g prunes, pitted
1 tablespoon coffee liqueur (such as Tia
    Maria or Sabra)

150g pecan halves
200g marzipan
250g dark cooking chocolate

Boil the prunes in a little water to soften. Drain and puree. Stir through the coffee liqueur and the pecans. Roll the marzipan into ½cm balls and set aside. Divide the prune mixture into four. Place ¼ onto baking paper and fashion into a log. Scatter half the marzipan balls evenly over the log and cover with another ¼ prune puree, ensuring the shape remains intact. Repeat the process for the second log. Freeze for 30 minutes.

Melt chocolate over a double boiler. Smooth a small amount of chocolate over the top of both logs and allow to set for a few minutes. Turn the logs over onto a new piece of baking paper and cover the other sides of the logs with chocolate. Refrigerate until ready to serve and slice into rounds.

(MAKES 2 LOGS)

Home-made
Pure chocolate
€5,00 /250gr

€20 /kg

*Markets everywhere —
always a sensory experience*

VIVIAN SCHENKER

Vivian Schenker is a journalist and media personality.

She was born in 1958 in Sydney, Australia. Her parents John and Emma fled Europe before World War II and Vivian grew up in a close-knit Jewish family. She graduated from Sydney University in 1979 and that year began her career as a cadet journalist at the ABC.

Vivian has worked in journalism, television and radio, producing and presenting documentaries, news and current affairs with extensive international experience. She was renowned as a host for ABC Radio National's *Breakfast*, Triple J, and SBS television. In recent years she was the deputy director of the Australian Labor Party's media and communications unit and is currently the national media advisor to the Australian Red Cross. Personal highlights include her trip to Nairobi to attend the End of the Decade for Woman Conference in 1985, and a successful documentary, *Penguins, Pingpong and Packice*, set in Antarctica.

Vivian lives in Sydney. With sport a favourite pastime, she claims to be a true armchair sportswoman. She loves to spend time with her family, cook, and go to the movies.

Blending In

My grandparents were pastry cooks. In fact, as a young man my grandfather travelled around Europe, learning a different technique in each city – working with yeast pastry, bread, sugar, chocolate. Before coming to Australia they owned a highly regarded *Konditorei* in Vienna (where they truly understand cake!).

After a few years in Australia, my grandparents established what they claimed to be the first such cake shop in Sydney. At first they predominantly baked finger buns, jam tarts and lamingtons, but as their clientele became more sophisticated, they were soon famous for their cream-cheese pockets, strudel and streusel.

My earliest and happiest memories are of Sunday afternoon teas at their big old house in Bondi, and the baking days that preceded them – my grandfather producing trays of perfect plaited little bread rolls covered in poppy-seeds for his adored grandchildren and my grandmother in her big white apron stuffing the yeast pastries with poppy seeds, walnuts or the thick sticky plum conserve known as *povidl*.

But like all children, I guess, I went through a phase of developing strange food tastes when I longed to be like all my Anglo friends, blending in by eating, speaking and thinking just like them. I was eight at the time. I'll never forget my grandmother's expression when she asked me what I'd like her to make for my special birthday dinner. 'Meat pies,' I said.

'OK,' she said, 'I'll make you a goulash and encase it in home-made pastry. It'll be delicious!'

'No, no, no,' I said, 'I want *bought* meat pies – the square ones you buy at the shop with tomato sauce.'

I thought she was going to faint, but she continued, 'And your birthday cake?'

'Chocolate with chocolate icing,' I said.

'Great,' my grandmother replied, more cheerfully, 'I'll make you a *Sachertorte* with *pariser* crème, a delicious mixture of dark chocolate and cream for the uninitiated.'

'No,' I insisted, 'I want the White Wings Chocolate packet cake, the one with the sachet of pre-mixed chocolate frosting.'

Now, I adored my grandmother, and I have to say she adored me; in later years we could discuss *everything*, including sex and relationships, but during that time the lines of communication were down.

Although she bought me the meat pie and made up the packet chocolate cake, for that brief period she had no idea who I was or where I was coming from. But by the time I turned nine, I had come to my senses!

My Grandmother Mitzi's Chocolate Cake

Every child's wish

4 eggs, separated
180g unsalted butter, softened
180g caster sugar
125g chocolate, melted
1 teaspoon vanilla essence
125g self-raising flour, sifted

GLAZE
250g cooking chocolate
120g unsalted butter

Preheat oven to 180°C. Grease and line 20cm cake tin.

Make cake: Cream butter and sugar until creamy and pale in colour. Beat in egg yolks, stir in melted chocolate, vanilla and then the flour. Beat egg whites until stiff, gently fold into the mixture and pour into the prepared tin. Bake for 40–45 minutes. Turn onto wire rack to cool.

Make glaze: Melt chocolate and butter together. Allow to cool to lukewarm temperature. Cover the cake with the warm glaze and leave to set before serving.

(SERVES 8)

Michael Steinhardt
is an American
businessman and
philanthropist active
in Jewish causes.

MICHAEL
STEINHARDT

He was born in 1940 in Brooklyn, New York, to Claire Deskin and Sol Steinhardt.

Finishing high school at age 16, he completed his studies at the Wharton School of Finance in three years, graduating in 1960, and then served in the US Army.

Michael began his career on Wall Street as an analyst. In 1967 he founded a hedge fund with Howard Berkowitz and Jerrold Fine – Steinhardt, Fine, Berkowitz & Co. – a pioneer in this field.

When Berkowitz and Fine left the partnership in 1979, the company became Steinhardt Partners LP. In 1995, at the age of 54 and with a career entirely focused on the world of money management, Michael suddenly announced his retirement and the closure of his successful hedge fund in order to devote his time to philanthropic causes.

Michael strongly supports cultural Jewish identity and continuity and has donated millions to this vision. In 1994 he set up the Steinhardt Foundation for Jewish Life with many programs to revitalise the infrastructure of American Jewish life, focusing on the future of Jewish youth. Michael and Charles Bronfman founded Taglit-Birthright Israel, a program that has allowed over 180,000 young adults from around the world aged 18–26 to visit Israel on a fully subsidised ten-day trip.

His generosity has extended to many other areas. Michael donated two islands – Steeple Jason Island and Grand Jason Island in the Falkland archipelago, which he owned – to the Bronx Zoo's Wildlife Conservation Society. His gifts to many universities are numerous and the Steinhardt School of Culture, Education and Human Development at New York University bears his name in acknowledgement of his generosity. He serves on many boards and committees.

In 2001 Michael published a biography, *No Bull: My Life in Markets*, which describes his life as a self-made man and his reasons for using his wealth for philanthropy. He is an avid art collector with a keen interest in artefacts, and apart from his family, his Westchester 'garden' is one of his greatest passions.

Michael lives in New York with his wife, Judy. They have three children, David, Daniel and Sara, and many grandchildren.

Chicken Fat Heaven

New York is a mecca for food lovers. It's difficult to nominate my favourite places but two restaurants in particular have special meaning for me.

One is called Sammy's Rumanian, situated on Chrystie Street on the Lower East Side in what used to be a very, very Jewish immigrant neighbourhood in Manhattan. You walk down four or five steps and enter a sub-level grungy environment. The walls are adorned with photographs of famous entertainers, movie stars, Jewish people from the stage, past guests and business cards stuck to picture frames. They have entertainment – old Jewish vaudeville types and Jewish music that one typically hears at weddings or bar or batmitzvahs; they even have a dance floor.

It is not a kosher restaurant but specialises in capturing what was a certain type of Jewish food in the 20th century. Sammy's signature dish is the Rumanian tenderloin, a skirt steak tenderised with minced garlic that is so generous it hides the plate! The menu is a cornucopia of delights to remind us of our Jewish roots, and includes chopped liver, stuffed cabbage, potato *latkes* with apple sauce, *kishke, kreplach, kasha varnishkes,* fried onions, mashed potatoes and *gribenes* (crisp fried chicken or goose skin cracklings). But the *pièce de résistance* is the table-top condiment – the melted chicken fat (*schmaltz*) in syrup bottles that allows you to add extra chicken fat to your food. You cannot imagine a food that is less good for you and has more cholesterol and fat!

Sammy's Rumanian serves a distinctive New York Jewish candy-store drink that every Jew above the age of fifty who grew up in New York knows intimately – egg cream. It is made with seltzer (soda water) from real old-fashioned seltzer bottles, a bottle of Fox's U-bet Chocolate Syrup and milk that you prepare at your table.

I used to go to Sammy's when I was young, then I took my children when *they* were young, and now sometimes my grandchildren also eat there.

Barney Greengrass – The Sturgeon King – is another wonderful New York restaurant with almost a 100-year character where you can savour the epicurean delights of our heritage – its raison d'être is its smoked fish. In my view, it has the best smoked fish anywhere in New York. The sturgeon is nirvana: so good and so sweet. Barney Greengrass has many different menu items that are distinct, and that make my mouth water when I think of them. It also has the best baked salmon and the best Nova Scotia salmon. As well as this, the deli is famous for its pastrami salmon, gravlax, kippered fish, caviar, *lox* and many other typical New York Jewish deli foods. I could go on and on …!

One can never go hungry in New York – in fact, I believe you could live there for years and never eat in the same restaurant twice. It really is a foodie's paradise!

New York Egg-Cream

Only in New York ... there are no eggs and no cream!

**2 tablespoons U-bet Chocolate Syrup, or
if unavailable, a good quality chocolate
syrup**
2 tablespoons milk
200ml soda water/seltzer, well chilled

Spoon the chocolate syrup into a tall chilled glass (250ml) and add the milk. Pour the cold soda water over the back of a spoon into the glass to within 2½ cm of the top. This will make a nice foamy chocolate head. Using a long spoon, stir the drink vigorously to mix the syrup and milk into a soda foam. Drink!

(MAKES 1 DRINK)

above: *Vivian Schenker with her grandparents, Mitzi and Otto.*

right: *Judy Kempler's parents, Evi and Felix.*

middle right: *Ian Bersten on a family holiday (centre).*

left: Madeleine Kunin as a young girl.

below left: Madeleine Kunin's parents, Ferdinand and Renée.

below right: Ian Bersten, aged three.

Celebration Fruit Slice

2 packets Morning Coffee, Tennis
    biscuits or plain sweet biscuits
250g butter
¾ cup brown sugar
2 eggs, beaten
2 tablespoons brandy
250g mixed dried fruit
100g slivered almonds

ICING
2 cups icing sugar
1 lemon, juiced
boiling water

Lightly grease a serving tray or platter.

Cover the platter or tray with a single layer of biscuits, depending on the size of the tray, in rows of 4 x 4 or 5 x 5 or 4 x 5 and without any space between the biscuits.

Crush remaining biscuits and set aside. Place butter and sugar in a saucepan and heat until butter is melted and sugar dissolved. Remove from heat. When just cool, stir in beaten eggs and brandy. Add dried fruit, almonds and crushed biscuits and mix well. Whilst still soft, gently spread this mixture over the prepared biscuit base, taking care not to separate the base. Refrigerate until set.

Make icing: Just before serving, mix icing sugar and lemon juice with enough water to achieve a thick consistency, and drizzle over the slice. Allow to set.

Cut into biscuit sizes in squares or diamonds at the table in front of the guests or just prior to serving.

Viola's Marzipan & Strawberry Diamonds

4 large eggs

60g dark chocolate

5 tablespoons caster sugar

¼ cup black coffee, fresh or instant
    dissolved in water

120g marzipan meal or superfine
    almond meal

1–2 teaspoons instant coffee granules

300ml single cream

1 x 250g punnet fresh strawberries,
    hulled and halved

Preheat oven to 180°C.

Line base and sides of 23cm square cake tin with baking paper.

Melt the dark chocolate over a double boiler and set aside to cool. Separate eggs.

Beat yolks with sugar until very light and fluffy. Add chocolate, black coffee and marzipan meal and mix well.

In a separate bowl, beat whites until stiff. Gently fold into chocolate mixture and pour into prepared tin.

Bake for approximately 35 minutes, until an inserted skewer comes out clean. Allow to cool completely.

Gently stir coffee granules into cream and whip until stiff. Cover cake with cream and cut into diamonds.

Decorate each diamond with a strawberry half.

(MAKES 20 SMALL SLICES)

Rosé Jelly with Mixed Berries

300g frozen mixed berries
1 x 85g sachet strawberry or raspberry
jelly crystals

1½ cups boiling water
¼ cup rosé wine

Place berries into a medium-sized clear glass bowl or into 6 individual clear glass dishes.
Place the jelly crystals in a separate bowl, pour over the boiling water and stir well to dissolve. Gently stir in rosé. Cool but do not allow to set. Pour jelly over the fruit and set in the refrigerator.

Note: This can be made the day before serving.

(SERVES 6)

~

Date & Ginger Balls

250g butter
1 cup white sugar
250g dried pitted dates, roughly
    chopped
1 egg, lightly beaten

1 teaspoon ground ginger
250g packet Marie biscuits or plain
    sweet biscuits, crushed
1 cup desiccated coconut

Melt butter and sugar in a saucepan over medium heat. Add dates and stir for 3 minutes or until mixture turns into a pulp. Add egg and ginger and continue to stir well. Remove from heat and mix in the biscuits. Set aside until cool to the touch. Roll into little balls and coat in coconut. Refrigerate.

(MAKES 36 SMALL BALLS)

Fruit Galette

1 sheet ready rolled puff pastry
450g fruit*, peeled and sliced
1 tablespoon brown sugar

1 tablespoon apricot or plum jam,
  warmed and strained
icing sugar, to garnish

Preheat oven to 200°C.

Place pastry on a lightly greased oven tray. Fold over edges to form a 1–2cm border. Arrange fruit on top in a single layer with the slices just overlapping and sprinkle sugar on top. Bake for 15 minutes until pastry is golden. Brush hot galette with warmed jam. Serve in slices, sprinkled with icing sugar.

* A variety of fruits may be used – pears, apples, peaches, nectarines, plums.
• If using pears or apples, toss gently in a little lemon juice and caster sugar to prevent browning.
• If using peaches or plums, place unpeeled fruit into boiling water for 1 minute, until skins can be peeled off easily.

(MAKES 4–6 SLICES)

~

Ginger Snaps

2 cups sugar
6 cups plain flour, sifted (extra may
  be needed)
2 teaspoons bicarbonate of soda

3 tablespoons ground ginger
250g butter, softened
2 eggs, well beaten
500g golden syrup

Preheat oven to 200°C. Grease and line baking trays.

Mix flour, bicarbonate of soda and ginger in a large bowl. Blend in butter. Add eggs and golden syrup. Mix well until the dough is very stiff, adding a little extra flour if dough is not very stiff.

Roll into walnut-sized balls, place on baking trays and gently flatten with a fork.

Bake until light brown in colour.

Note: The ingredients can be halved for a smaller quantity.

(MAKES 100 BISCUITS)

Nana's Custard Biscuits

120g custard powder
120g icing sugar mixture (not pure icing sugar)

360g plain flour
360g butter
100 choc bits (milk or dark)

Preheat oven to 180°C. Grease or line oven trays with baking paper.

Place all ingredients, except choc bits, into a bowl and rub together, then knead to form a soft dough.

Roll into small balls (about 1.5cm) and place on baking trays.

Slightly flatten each ball by gently pressing down with a fork.

Push a choc bit into the centre of each ball.

Bake for 8–10 minutes, until the base of each biscuit just begins to turn golden (do not over bake).

(MAKES ABOUT 100 SMALL BISCUITS)

Rocky Road

150g marshmallows, pink, white or
    a mixture
90g glacé cherries (Turkish Delight or
    dried apricots can be substituted)

500g milk, white or dark chocolate
45g crushed peanuts or almonds

Line 11cm x 22cm tin or similarly sized container with foil or baking paper.

Chop marshmallows and cherries into quarters and set aside. Melt chocolate over very low heat, stirring occasionally. Spread approximately ⅓ melted chocolate over the base of the tin. Layer half the marshmallows, glacé cherries and nuts over the chocolate. Spread half the remaining chocolate over this. Lay remaining marshmallows, cherries and nuts over chocolate and then spread remaining chocolate on top. Refrigerate to set for approximately 8 hours. Remove foil or paper, cut into small squares and refrigerate in airtight container.

(MAKES APPROX. 20 PIECES)

~

Mini Florentines

1 cup raisins
1 cup mixed dried fruit
1¼ cups corn flakes
1¼ cups unsalted peanuts, pecans
    or almonds

10 extra glacé cherries, cut into quarters
1 x 395g tin sweetened condensed milk
200g cooking chocolate, milk or dark,
    melted

Preheat oven to 150°C. Line baking tray with baking paper.

Combine all ingredients except chocolate. Place heaped teaspoons of the mixture onto the baking tray. Bake for 10–15 minutes, watching that the biscuits do not burn. Remove from oven and cool. When florentines are cold, spread the flat side of each with melted chocolate, using a fork to make wavy patterns. Leave to set.

(MAKES APPROX. 20 PIECES)

A CHILDHOOD TASTE LASTS FOREVER
Pnina Jacobson

'Come Nini, come watch me.' Solly lifted me onto the counter-top and began creating. Using piping cream, glacé cherries and sprinkles, his strong hands could turn a simple pudding into a gastronomic delight. I watched him boil and bake bagels and prepare all the Jewish dishes my mother had taught him.

Amidst all this, two other pots were boiling away on the stove. In one pot was a staple African food called *pap* made from corn maize or *mealie* meal. In the other pot was a tomato-based sauce.

When Solly had cleaned up the kitchen, he lifted the two pots off the stove, turned to me and said, 'Come, we eat.' I jumped off the counter-top and followed him outside. Although the sky was a beautiful blue, the air was crisp and the grass burnt from the frost that falls during the Highveld winter. Solly sat down on a large stone and I sat cross-legged on the dry grass, anticipating lunch. He slowly raised the lids of the pots, the steam disappearing into the nippy air. Solly put his hand into the *pap* pot and pulled out a small amount, then he moulded the pliable *pap* into a ball and handed it to me. I blew onto the hot *pap* and dipped it gingerly into the sauce. 'Hmm,' I said.

Today, I serve *pap* and sauce to accompany meat at our BBQs, fondly remembering my wonderful moments with Solly, our African cook, and the delicious taste of his cooking.

'Come Nini, come watch me.' Solly lifted me onto the counter-top and began creating.

ABOUT THE AUTHORS

Pnina Jacobson was born in the farming community of Bethal, South Africa. Her late father Sam (Adler), a Hebrew teacher, married her mother Rhona (Hirschowitz), whose family were established farmers in the region. Sam and Rhona set up their own farm, growing large crops of corn and potatoes for sale at the Johannesburg markets. Pnina had a wonderful childhood with her brother Frank and sister Daphne, and her love of fresh food stems from these early years in which cousins, family and friends would gather on the farm to share many memorable meals. Pnina moved to Cape Town to work as a pre-school teacher and shortly after married Ivor. They immigrated to Sydney, Australia, in 1987 and Pnina continued her work as a pre-school teacher. She furthered her studies in Jewish history while raising her first child. Each aspect of this book is a labour of love, especially her friendship with Judy. Pnina continues to help Ivor in his dental practices while raising her children Sam, Danielle and Laura.

Judy Kempler was born and raised in Sydney, Australia. She enjoyed a carefree and happy, surrounded by her parents, Evi and Felix (Lewin), brother, Bob, an exceptionally close-knit extended family and friends. From sharing picnics, boating trips on the Hawkesbury to holidays in the snow and Blue Mountains to sharing celebrations, a fundamental ingredient was good home-made food. Judy's profession in the IT industry allowed her to work while raising a young family. Career opportunities for her husband John lead to an exciting life in Melbourne and Singapore. On returning home, Judy helped care for her elderly mother-in-law Viola (Kempler); this experience drew her attention to the ever-growing needs of the aged in the community. The publication of this book *One Egg Is A Fortune* is the realisation of a personal dream: combining an interest in Jewish history and food with a charitable cause while remaining a stay-at-home mum. Through this, Pnina and Judy developed a very special camaraderie... sitting for hours, telephoning, writing, laughing, cooking and the sharing of this journey. Judy and John live in Sydney and have three children, Steven, Jacqui and Lise.

CONVERSION TABLES

Oven Temperatures

DESCRIPTION	CELSIUS (ELECTRIC)	CELSIUS (FAN- FORCED)	FAHRENHEIT	GAS MARK
Very Slow	120	100	250	½
-	140	120	285	1
Slow	150	130	300	2
Moderately slow	160	140	320	3
Moderate	180	160	350	4
-	190	170	375	5
Moderately hot	200	180	400	6
Hot	220	200	425	7
-	230	210	450	8
Very hot	240	220	475	9

Spoon measurements

¼ teaspoon	1.25ml
½ teaspoon	2.5ml
1 teaspoon	5ml
1 tablespoon (AUS)	20ml (4 teaspoons)
1 tablespoon (UK/US)	15ml (3 teaspoons)

Metric cup & spoon sizes

CUP	METRIC
¼ cup	60ml
⅓ cup	80ml
½ cup	125ml
1 cup	250ml

SPOON	METRIC
¼ teaspoon	1.25ml
½ teaspoon	2.5ml
1 teaspoon	5ml
2 teaspoons	10ml
1 tablespoon (equal to 4 teaspoons)	20ml

Cake Pan measurements

20cm springform cake pan	8 inch
20cm square cake pan	8 inch
23cm springform cake pan	9 inch
25cm springform cake pan	10 inch

Liquids

METRIC	CUP	IMPERIAL
30ml		1 fl oz
60ml	¼ cup	2 fl oz
80ml		3 ½ fl oz
100ml	⅓ cup	2 ¾ fl oz
125ml	½ cup	4 fl oz
150ml		5 fl oz
180ml	¾ cup	6 fl oz
200ml		7 fl oz
250ml	1 cup	8 ¾ fl oz
310ml	1 ¼ cups	10 ½ fl oz
375ml	1 ½ cups	13 fl oz
430ml	1 ¾ cups	15 fl oz
475ml		16 fl oz
500ml	2 cups	17 fl oz
625ml	2 ½ cups	21 ½ fl oz
750ml	3 cups	26 fl oz
1L	4 cups	35 fl oz
1.25L	5 cups	44 fl oz
1.5L	6 cups	52 fl oz
2L	8 cups	70 fl oz
2.5L	10 cups	88 fl oz

Mass (weight)

10g	¼oz
15g	½oz
30g	1oz
60g	2oz
90g	3oz
125g	4oz (¼ lb)
155g	5oz
185g	6oz
220g	7oz
250g	8oz (½ lb)
280g	9oz
315g	10oz
345g	11oz
375g	12oz (¾ lb)
410g	13oz
440g	14oz
470g	15oz
500g (½ kg)	16oz (1 lb)
750g	24oz (1 ½ lb)
1kg	32oz (2 lb)
1.5kg	48oz (3 lb)
2kg	64oz (4 lb)

Food Name Equivalents

plain flour	all-purpose flour
caster sugar	superfine sugar
icing sugar	powdered sugar
bicarbonate of soda	baking soda
corn flour	corn starch
mince	ground meat
golden syrup	light corn syrup
capsicum	bell pepper
coriander	cilantro leaves
eggplant	aubergine
flat-leaf parsley	Italian/continental parsley
rocket leaves	arugula leaves
zucchini	courgette
spring onion	scallion or green onion
double or rich cream	heavy cream (45–48% fat)
pure or regular or single cream	whipping cream (35–40% fat)

These conversions have been rounded up for cookery purposes

PHOTO CREDITS

Cover and recipe photography by Craig Cranko.

P2:	Photo by Craig Cranko.
P9:	© iStockphoto.com/Alex Kokoulin, centre.
P9:	Other photos by Ivor Jacobson and Steven Kempler
P10:	Photo by Craig Cranko.
P14:	Photo courtesy of George Dreyfus.
P18:	Photo courtesy of Tovah Feldshuh.
P22:	Photo by Guntar Kravis, courtesy of Deb Filler.
P26–27:	Photos by Craig Cranko, Sam Jacobson and Lise Kempler.
P28–30:	Photos courtesy of Yossi Ghinsberg.
P34:	Photo by Steve Wood, courtesy of UAB.
P36:	Photo courtesy of Rhona Adler.
P40:	Photo courtesy of Lord Janner.
P44:	Photo by Frédéric Brenner, courtesy of Barbara Kirshenblatt-Gimblatt.
P49:	© iStockphoto.com/Darieus, top right.
P49:	© iStockphoto.com/2ndLookGraphics, bottom right.
P48–49:	Other photos by Jacqui Kempler and Judy Kempler.
P50:	Photo courtesy of Marc Salem.
P54-55:	Cartoon © Art Spiegelman.
P56:	Photo by Judy Kempler.
P60:	Photo by Branco Gaica, courtesy of TML Enterprises.
P64–65:	Photo of Chaim Topol by Branco Gaica, courtesy of TML Enterprises; photo of Barbara Kirshenblatt-Gimblatt with Mayer Kirshenblatt by Frédéric Brenner; paintings courtesy of Barbara Kirshenblatt-Gimblatt, reprinted from *They Called Me Mayer July: Painted Memories of a Jewish Childhood in Poland Before the Holocaust* (Berkeley: University of California Press, 2007); photo of Tovah Feldshuh as Golda by Aaron Epstein; musical score and photo courtesy of George Dreyfus; photo courtesy of Lord Janner.
P68:	Photos by Laura Jacobson and Lise Kempler.
P71:	Photos by Ivor Jacobson and Steven Kempler.
P76:	Photo by Ingrid Shakenovsky, courtesy of Joanne Fedler.
P78:	Photo and recipe courtesy of Joanne Fedler.
P82:	Photo by Judy Kempler.
P84:	Photos courtesy of Gavin Fingleson.
P88:	Photo courtesy of Gary Friedman.
P92:	Photo by Judy Kempler.
P94:	Photo courtesy of Alan Gold; other photos courtesy of David Kendler.
P98:	© iStockphoto.com/sfmthd, top left.
P99:	© iStockphoto.com/LanceB, bottom left.
P98–99:	Other photos by Ivor Jacobson and Judy Kempler.
P100:	Photo courtesy of Gillian Helfgott.
P104:	Photo by Jennie Cruse, courtesy of Herschal Herscher.
P108:	Photo courtesy of Ron Klinger.
P112:	Photo courtesy of Lenny Krayzelburg.
P116:	Photo courtesy of Brian Sherman.
P120:	© iStockphoto.com/JJMaree, bottom.
P121:	© iStockphoto.com/Sukikaki, top.
P121:	© iStockphoto.com/RapidEye, middle.
P121:	© iStockphoto.com/belterz, bottom left.
P121 :	© iStockphoto.com/jaap-willem, bottom right.
P120–121:	Other photos by Ivor Jacobson and Judy Kempler.
P122:	Photo courtesy Tali Shine Pty Ltd.
P126:	Dan Hubig/San Francisco Chronicle (C) 2011.
P128:	Photos by Ivor Jacobson.
P132:	Photo by Jillian Edelstein, courtesy of Janet Suzman.
P136–137:	Photos courtesy of Gary Friedman; Gillian and David Helfgott; Tali Shine; Herschal Herscher; Brian Sherman; photos of Janet Suzman as a child and as Cleopatra by Reg Wilson, courtesy of Janet Suzman; photo of Shanghai by Ivor Jacobson.
P140:	Photos by Ivor Jacobson and Lise Kempler.
P149:	Photos by Ivor Jacobson and Lise Kempler.
P152:	Photo by Judy Kempler.
P156–157:	Photos by Ivor Jacobson and Jacqui Kempler.
P158-160:	Photo of Neshama with her late father Rabbi Shlomo Carlebach by Joan Roth; all photos courtesy of Neshama Carlebach.
P164:	Photo by Yona Verwer, courtesy of Phyllis Chesler.
P168:	Photo courtesy of Aviva Rosenfeld.
P172:	Photo by Bachrach Studio, courtesy of Alan Dershowitz.
P176:	Photo courtesy of The Israel Project.
P180:	Photo by Igor Bass, courtesy of Dudu Fisher.
P184:	Photo courtesy of Gil Hovav.
P186:	© iStockphoto.com/Aron Brand.
P190:	Photo by Michael Silver, courtesy of Sam Lipski.
P 195:	© iStockphoto.com/lucylui, top right.
P195:	© iStockphoto.com/attator, bottom left.
P194–195:	Other photos by Ivor Jacobson and Steven Kempler.
P196:	Photo courtesy of Washington Institute for Near East Policy.
P200:	Photo by Francine Davita, courtesy of Ethan Zohn.
P204–205:	Photos courtesy of Alan Crown; Rabbi Shmuley Boteach; Phyllis Chesler; Dudu Fisher; Rhona Adler; Ethan Zohn.
P211:	Photos by Ivor Jacobson and Judy Kempler.
P214:	Photos by Ivor Jacobson and Judy Kempler.
P218–220:	Photos courtesy of the Great Synagogue, Sydney.
P224:	Photo courtesy of Ian Bersten.
P228–230:	Photo of Max Brenner by Tess Steinkolk; all photos courtesy of Max Brenner.
P234–236:	Photo of Judy Cassab by Judy Kempler; all photos courtesy of Judy Cassab.
P240–241:	Photos by Ivor Jacobson, Steven Kempler and Seb Ruiz.
P242:	Photo courtesy of New Israel Fund.
P246:	Photo courtesy of Anthony Glass.

P250–252: Photo of Hirsh Goodman by Esteban Alterman; all photos courtesy of Hirsh Goodman.

P256–258: Photo of Ruth Hendel by Liana Ferris. Photos courtesy of Ruth Hendel and Jacqui Kempler.

P258: © iStockphoto.com/ericsphotography, top.

P262: Photo courtesy of the Brookings Institution.

P266: Photo by Karen Heath, Kaz Photography, courtesy of Rachael Kohn.

P269: Plate provided by Will Braat, John Braat and Company (www.johnbraat.com).

P270: Photo by Paul Boisvert, courtesy of Madeleine Kunin.

P274: Photo courtesy of Naomi Leibler.

P278: Photo courtesy of Max Markson.

P282: Photo by Jonathan Exley, courtesy of Marlee Matlin.

P286: Photo by Judy Kempler.

P290–291: Photos by Sam Jacobson and Lise Kempler.

P292: Photo by Judy Kempler.

P296: Photo courtesy of Steinhardt Management LLC.

P300–301: Photos courtesy of Vivian Schenker; Madeleine Kunin; Ian Bersten; Evi Lewin.

P303: Photos by Lise Kempler and Seb Ruiz.

P306: Photos by Ivor Jacobson and Lise Kempler.

P 308: © iStockphoto.com/turanj, left.

P 308: © iStockphoto.com/gertfrik, middle.

P 308: © iStockphoto.com/NikeAlberts, right.

P309: Photos by Ivor Jacobson and Steven Kempler.

P319: Photo by Craig Cranko.

WEBSITES TO NOTE

Rabbi Raymond Apple: www.oztorah.com

Ian Bersten: www.tea-cha.com.au

Rabbi Shmuley Boteach: www.shmuley.com

Max Brenner: www.maxbrenner.com.au

Neshama Carlebach: www.neshamacarlebach.com

Judy Cassab: www.judycassab.com

Phyllis Chesler: www.phyllis-chesler.com

Alan Dershowitz: www.alandershowitz.com

Joanne Fedler: www.joannefedler.com

Tovah Feldshuh: www.tovahfeldshuh.com

Deb Filler: www.fillerup.ca

Gavin Fingleson: www.o2studio.com.au

Dudu Fisher: www.dudufisher.com

Gary Friedman: www.puppetrynews.com

Yossi Ghinsberg: www.ghinsberg.com

Sharon Glass: www.sharonsrecipes.co.za

David Helfgott: www.davidhelfgott.com

Herschal Herscher: www.jewsbrothers.com

Donna Jacobs-Sife: www.donnajacobsife.com

Lord Janner of Braunstone: www.grevillejanner.org.uk

Lenny Krayzelburg: www.lennykswim.com

Madeleine Kunin: www.madeleinekunin.org

Isi and Naomi Leibler: www.wordfromjerusalem.com

Sam Lipski: www.samlipski.com

Max Markson: www.marksonsparks.com.au

Marlee Matlin: www.marleematlinsite.com

Dennis Ross: www.dennisross.house.gov

Marc Salem: www.marcsalem.com

Brian Sherman: www.voiceless.org.au

Tali Shine: www.talishine.com

Marlena Spieler: www.marlenaspieler.com

Michael Steinhardt: www.jewishlife.org

Ethan Zohn: www.ezohn.com

THE FOLLOWING MATERIAL HAS BEEN REPRINTED WITH PERMISSION

P45: Extract from *They Called Me Mayer July: Painted Memories of a Jewish Childhood in Poland Before the Holocaust* by Barbara Kirshenblatt-Gimblett and Mayer Kirshenblatt, reprinted with permission of University of California Press.

P54: Cartoon by Art Spiegelman reprinted with permission of Art Spiegelman.

P61: Extract from *Topol by Topol* (Weidenfeld and Nicolson, 1981) and *To Life! A Treasury of Wit and Humour* (Robson Books, 1994) with permission of Chaim Topol.

P109: Extract from Ron Klinger's *The Bridge Player Who Laughed* (Modern Bridge Publications, 1994) with permission of Ron Klinger.

P127-129: Extracts from *The Roving Feast* (San Francisco Chronicle, 2004 and 2005) with permission of Marlena Spieler.

P202: Recipe *Blazing Hot Wing Sauce with Beer* reprinted with permission of John Schlimm, author of *The Ultimate Beer Lover's Cookbook*.

P232: Recipe *Rich Chocolate Truffles* adapted from *Favourite Chocolate Recipes by the Bald Man* (2007) with permission of Max Brenner.

P251-253: Extract from *Let Me Create A Paradise, G-d Said to Himself* by Hirsh Goodman reprinted with permission of Hirsh Goodman.

P279: Anecdote from Max Markson adapted from Max Markson's *Show Me The Money* (Viking, Penguin Books Australia, 2000) and used with permission of Max Markson.

INDEX

ONE EGG IS A FORTUNE

ONE EGG IS A FORTUNE
Published in 2011 by One Egg is a Fortune
www.oneeggisafortune.com

National Library of Australia Cataloguing-in-Publication Data
Authors: Pnina Jacobson and Judy Kempler
Title: One Egg is a Fortune
Publisher: One Egg is a Fortune
ISBN: 978-0-9871577-0-6
Subjects: Cooking
Dewey Number: 641.5

Food Photography by Craig Cranko
Food Styling by Michele Cranston
Editing by Nadine Davidoff
Design by i2i Design pty ltd
Pre-press by Colour Chiefs
Printed by 1010 printing

It is the intention of the publishers that part of the proceeds from sales of the book will be donated to organisations in Australia, the United States and elsewhere which provide aged care services to the Jewish populations in those communities.

One Egg is a Fortune can be purchased directly via www.oneeggisafortune.com